I Golf,
Therefore I Am—
NUTS!

I Golf,
Therefore I Am—

George Fuller

Illustrated by
Joe Jahraus

Human Kinetics

Library of Congress Cataloging-in-Publication Data

Fuller, George, 1954-
  I golf, therefore I am--nuts! / George Fuller.
    p. cm.
  Includes bibliographical references.
  ISBN-13: 978-0-7360-7528-2 (soft cover)
  ISBN-10: 0-7360-7528-3 (soft cover)
  1. Golf--Anecdotes. 2. Golf--Humor. I. Title.
  GV967.F86 2009
  796.352--dc22

                          2008032585

ISBN-10: 0-7360-7528-3 (print)   ISBN-10: 0-7360-7940-8 (Kindle)
ISBN-13: 978-0-7360-7528-2 (print)   ISBN-13: 978-0-7360-7940-2 (Kindle)

ISBN-10: 0-7360-7939-4 (Mobipocket)   ISBN-10: 0-7360-8112-7 (Adobe PDF)
ISBN-13: 978-0-7360-7939-6 (Mobipocket) ISBN-13: 978-0-7360-8112-2 (Adobe PDF)

The Web addresses cited in this text were current as of August 2008, unless otherwise noted.

Acquisitions Editor: Tom Heine; **Developmental Editor:** Heather Healy; **Assistant Editor:** Carla Zych; **Copyeditor:** Tom Tiller; **Proofreader:** Jim Burns; **Permission Manager:** Martha Gullo; **Graphic Designer:** Joe Buck; **Graphic Artist:** Tara Welsch; **Cover Designer:** Keith Blomberg; **Photo Office Assistant:** Jason Allen; **Art Manager:** Kelly Hendren; **Associate Art Manager:** Alan L. Wilborn; **Illustrator (cover and interior):** Joe Jahraus; **Printer:** Versa Press

Human Kinetics books are available at special discounts for bulk purchase. Special editions or book excerpts can also be created to specification. For details, contact the Special Sales Manager at Human Kinetics.

Printed in the United States of America   10   9   8   7   6   5   4   3   2   1

Human Kinetics
Web site: www.HumanKinetics.com

United States: Human Kinetics
P.O. Box 5076
Champaign, IL 61825-5076
800-747-4457
e-mail: humank@hkusa.com

Canada: Human Kinetics
475 Devonshire Road Unit 100
Windsor, ON N8Y 2L5
800-465-7301 (in Canada only)
e-mail: info@hkcanada.com

Europe: Human Kinetics
107 Bradford Road
Stanningley
Leeds LS28 6AT, United Kingdom
+44 (0) 113 255 5665
e-mail: hk@hkeurope.com

Australia: Human Kinetics
57A Price Avenue
Lower Mitcham, South Australia 5062
08 8372 0999
e-mail: info@hkaustralia.com

New Zealand: Human Kinetics
Division of Sports Distributors NZ Ltd.
P.O. Box 300 226 Albany
North Shore City
Auckland
0064 9 448 1207
e-mail: info@humankinetics.co.nz

For Landry, who is always adventurous enough
to play nine, wise enough to stop thereafter, and
understanding enough to let me slog on.

Contents

Acknowledgments   xiii
Please Don't Steal My Golf Ball   xv

Part I   The First Tee   1

Chapter 1   In the Beginning, There Was Golf..... 3

And it was good . . . and bad . . . and good . . .
and . . .

Chapter 2   Any Way You Slice It,
Golf Is a Beautiful Game.................. 7

Heads of state and the guy next door all bow down to
this glorious game.

Chapter 3   The Patron Saint of Forgiveness:
Seeking the Elusive Mulligan.......... 11

How rough roads and the Biltmore Hotel lead to golf's
most generous gesture.

Chapter 4   Couples Golf.............................. 15

Be sure the battle of the sexes doesn't diminish your
love or your love of the links.

Chapter 5   The Laws of Golf 19

Anything that can go wrong will go wrong—especially
on the golf course.

Chapter 6   Forget Love—
Laugh at the One You're With........ 25

Doubled over with laughter isn't a bad way to spend
an afternoon.

Part II The Power Game   29

Chapter 7   Desperately Seeking 3 Wood 31

We've come a long way, baby . . . or have we?

**Chapter 8   Making Fast Friends
on the Links** 35

Bonding over lasagna, literature, and a whole lot of liquor.

**Chapter 9   Hype Versus Reality—
Can You Believe This?** 39

The Augusta National of Texas and other tall tales.

**Chapter 10 The Game of the Future?
Let's Hope Not** 45

Course construction and sanity surge to the outer limits.

Chapter 11 No Pain, No Gain 51

Lessons in humility (and humiliation) from the few and the proud.

Part III The Short Game   55

Chapter 12 Putting Stroke Du Jour 57

A rolling boil may be your key to success.

Chapter 13 Practice Schmactice 61

Be prepared or be content with your handicap.

Chapter 14 Client Golf 65

Keeping your brownnose to the grind stone.

**Chapter 15 Golden Golf:
Till Death Do Us Part** 69

Hard of hearing and short of sight is a blissful way to play the game.

Chapter 16 Lucky Charms.............................73

Is luck a lady . . . or an acorn?

Part IV The Mental Game 77

Chapter 17 The Parboiled Language
of Golf 79

One person's jargon is another person's poetry.

Chapter 18 Weapons of Mass Instruction 83

When it comes to advice, sometimes less is more.

Chapter 19 Gamesmanship 87

Surreptitiously skirting the rules to get inside your
opponent's head.

Chapter 20 E9 91

Nine holes and a whale of a tale can set you right as
rain.

Chapter 21 The Tyranny of Par 95

Give me liberty or give me . . . a 1 iron!

Chapter 22 Remembering Why We Play...........99

How to turn your trash to treasure.

Chapter 23 Open Letter to the PGA Tour
Commissioner...........................103

Take this game and . . . well, you know.

Chapter 24 Leaps of Faith.............................109

Do a little dance, make another putt, this game's all
right!

Part V Course Management 113

Chapter 25 Golf or a Lime Exfoliation? 115

You pamper your way, and I'll pamper mine.

Chapter 26 March of the Haggis 119

No, really, I couldn't eat another bite.

Chapter 27 Shark Versus Bear 123

Golf course openings, sharks, and bears—oh my!

Chapter 28 Golf in the Middle
of Nowhere................................127

A golf course built from bird droppings?

Chapter 29 Travels With Dave 133

Then there was the time . . .

Chapter 30 Dreaming My Dreams.................137

A daydream believer and a tropical scene.

Chapter 31 Whipped by the Master—Again 141

My love-hate relationship with a classic course.

Part VI Tales From the Tour   145

Chapter 32 The Thrill of Victory—
Well, Almost 147

A course in international relations on the links.

Chapter 33 A Babe in Mastersland.................151

Predictions, picks, and professional pundits.

Chapter 34 A Primer on Golf Fashion 155

Some fashion plates were meant to be broken.

Chapter 35 How to Host a U.S. Open............159

Tailgating and tee times—a match made in heaven.

Chapter 36 Looking Down at the Grass..........163

One of golf's greats provides perspective on the game
and milkshakes.

Chapter 37 Whistling While You Work 169

Relax, stroll the fairways, and give a little whistle.

Chapter 38 Bada-Bing—A Proposal to Improve the AT&T Pebble Beach National Pro-Am by Changing That Way-Too-Long Name and Bringing Back the Spirit of Bing Crosby 173

My cause celeb: more professionals, please.

Part VII The 19th Hole 179

Chapter 39 Dog is My Copilot 181

How about a game of fetch on the green?

Chapter 40 Dew Sweepers, Diehards, and the Dearly Departed 185

Neither snow, nor rain, nor heat will stop these golfers.

Chapter 41 Dweezel and Chuckles Rip Me a Shred Stick 189

A couple of golfing groms snake my Sunday.

Chapter 42 My Favorite Excuse 193

The dog ate my homework and other reasons why my putting stinks.

Chapter 43 Top 10 New Year's Resolutions for Golfers 199

My diet and golf practice start tomorrow.

Chapter 44 The Power of the Pen 203

A humble golf writer's daydreams dissolve via a sibling rivalry reality check.

**Chapter 45 Beam Me Out of the Woods,
               Scotty** **211**

Golf gizmos and gadgets galore.

Afterword: My Next Book   217
Reference Points   221
About the Author   225
About the Illustrator   227

Acknowledgments

First and foremost, many thanks and much gratitude to my wife, Landry, who—even though she didn't think I was very funny at first—now laughs at me all the time. Well, I mean she laughs at my stories. Right, dear? We have established a ritual over the years we've been married, wherein she works for a living and I stay home with the dogs writing funny stories. That, my friends, is the big secret to being a golf writer: a spouse who works. When I finally harass her into coming home for the evening for dinner, the first thing I so unselfishly do (after giving her a big smooch for supporting the family) is thrust my manuscript into her hands, eagerly pointing out the piece I finished that day. I then sit there like a big dumb puppy while she reads it out loud, laughing at all the right places and adding nuance to all the right words and phrases.

If she stumbles over a passage as she recites it, I rewrite it the next day, and I edit the rest of the manuscript according to her other comments and suggestions, though I probably looked askance at her when she suggested them the previous night. That's just how we big dumb puppies work; it takes us a little while to process and acknowledge any feedback other than "My, you are so talented and wonderful. And did I mention good-looking?" In this tender and eternal way, Landry is my first and most important reader, and her patience, understanding, and laughter are forever cherished.

I'm sorry to say that this book contains just about everything I've learned about golf over the years, though undoubtedly I'll keep writing about the holy game for many years to come. Therefore, I must also acknowledge those many people who have endured my huge learning curve, including family members. First are my brother, David, and his wife, Edie, who, clearly, have put up with me only for the free golf. Then there are the many friends and colleagues (you know who you are, which is fantastic because I've mostly forgotten), and countless foursome mates who have shown amazing patience and understanding while I pretended to know pretty much everything about golf. And of course you, dear reader—I absolutely thank for your unquenchable thirst for golf knowledge.

I would also like to tip my logoed cap to all the creatures, great and small, that I've encountered on the golf courses of the world. They make golf a truly wonderful game. The two-legged ones are funniest, and many have contributed—mostly unknowingly and probably unwillingly, if they had a choice—to the tales printed herein. The many winged and four-legged ones—among them elk, deer, owls, bald eagles, coyotes, baby foxes, moose, alligators, donkeys, boars, and even those ornery little squirrels who claw your golf bag to shreds in search of food—have made golf courses among the most beautiful places in the world to hang out.

In closing, I cannot forget the three elderly gentlemen I played with last weekend at my home course. They typify and embody the spirit of this book, and I'd like to share the following conversation I overheard among them, since it brought a big smile to my face, as I hope it will to yours:

First one said, "Windy, isn't it?"

Second one said, "No, it's Thursday!"

Third one said, "So am I. Let's go get a beer."

And off they went. And off we go.

Please Don't Steal My Golf Ball

My earliest experiences on a golf course were mischievous, maybe even slightly criminal. When I was 7 or 8 years old, we lived across the street from a prestigious private golf course in Pacific Palisades, California. My older brother and I would entertain ourselves on Saturday mornings by hiding in the bushes next to one certain green, and when a ball landed near enough to where we were hiding, we'd take turns scurrying through a small hole we'd dug under the chain link fence, running onto the green, and stealing the ball.

The golfer whose shot had so elegantly flown into our realm of tomfoolery would yell at us from the fairway—"Hey, you! Put that down! Come back here!"—and start running toward us. When he arrived at the fence and saw the size of the hole we had wiggled under, he'd yell more about reporting us to the authorities and then stomp off to drop a ball and undoubtedly bogey the hole. Ha!

I don't have any of those warm and fuzzy stories you sometimes read about a father and his young son sharing quality time on the golf course: the father teaching the lad the fine points of the game, the son eventually improving to the point where he can finally beat the old man, and the two of them heading off to Scotland to play some sentimental rounds when the old man is on his last legs. I have none of those stories.

My dad was not a member of that course we lived next to; in fact, as far as I knew, he didn't play golf at all. I do remember a dusty leather bag of Wilson golf clubs in our garage. I figured they must have been my dad's, but they disappeared, undoubtedly unloaded at a garage sale on a smoggy Southern California Sunday in the 1970s. Too bad—they might have been worth something by now. Who knows, maybe he's taken up the game in the afterlife (we do sometimes refer to it as "the holy game"). If so, I hope he's teeing it up with Sam Snead or Jimmy Demaret, because I think he'd get along well with those two lions of the game.

It was not until I was in my mid-30s—with knees and ankles too weak to keep pace on the basketball court—that I came to play golf myself. But, as it is for so many of us, once I was smitten by the game, I was smitten hard. Whether you pronounce it *gaaf* as do our nasally Boston brothers and sisters, *gaawff* as do our cousins in the South, or *gooff* as it is pronounced in Scotland, it is a similar state of smittenness we share.

I discovered golf to be a truly great game, one that brings together all sorts of folk who otherwise would never meet, in circumstances where their manners are at their best—or at least should be. I've met some of the most interesting people ever on golf courses and played in some extraordinary surroundings: on top of an active volcano, through stands of towering redwood trees so thick it would take five people forming a human chain to get their arms around the trunks, past ponds with alligators sunning on the banks, and next to rattlesnakes when errant shots came to rest near them.

Of all these circumstances, it is only in the case of snakes or alligators that one benefits from a free drop, though two club lengths from a rattlesnake is not quite far enough for my comfort. Local rules in some parts of Florida and South Carolina give a 10-foot drop away from an alligator and recommend running in a zigzag line if one charges, since gators can only run straight. I have not cared to test that theory.

Redwoods are played as are any other tree, though one is inclined to hit somewhat more majestically from behind one. Lava? Well, you can hit out if you wish, but don't use your favorite 7 iron; it will end up looking like a spoon that's been down the drain when the garbage disposal was turned on, and the sound of hitting from it is not much prettier.

Personally, I prefer to take my drops and still have my wits about me to admire the views. Maybe Seamus McDuff of *Golf in the Kingdom* would scold me, but we're far from the Kingdom and close to the edge here in the provinces of golf. I say go for maximum pleasure: Don't anger the alligators or rattlesnakes—and whatever you do, don't anger yourself.

Go have fun. And please, if my golf ball happens to land on a green near you, don't steal it!

PART

I

The First Tee

In the Beginning, There Was Golf

Beginnings. That's what I love so much about the game of golf. No matter how well or poorly I played the last hole, I get a fresh start 18 times a round. That's double the lives of Morris the Cat!

Of course, golf is also about middles and endings, how well we hold up under pressure, how we react when we get a bad break we didn't deserve—or a good break we did. As celebrated author Rick Reilly once pointed out, "Like bike pants, golf tells you a lot about a person."

Do you crack when frustrated and fly off the edge of the world? (Remember, *golf* spelled backward is *flog*.) Or do you take poorly struck shots in stride, calmly chase your ball, and hit it again with a smile on your face? I've done both, but the latter is so much more satisfying than the former. And better for your blood pressure, too.

A 25-handicap friend of mine named Bob once told me about a certain day when he hacked and hewed his way around his home course in Atlanta:

"I was having the worst day I had ever had. I couldn't hit a thing. Nothing was working, and I kept getting madder and madder. Finally, about 150 yards out in the 16th fairway, I took a big whack at the ball with my 8 iron and hit the ground hard. The ball moved about 10 inches forward, and there was a deep, nasty gash in the turf staring up at me.

"That was it—I turned, flung my club into the woods and finished the hole with a putter. After the round I went back to get my 8 iron. When I found it, I saw that the club head had snapped off when it hit a tree and was nowhere to be found. So I took the shaft to the pro and asked him if he could straighten it and put a new head on it.

"'What happened?' the pro asked. 'I can send this back to the manufacturer. The club head shouldn't be falling off like that. It's obviously faulty.' So I told him how it happened. Suddenly his tune changed. 'Bob,' he said, 'you're a 25-handicap golfer—you're not good enough to get mad!'"

The light bulb came on in Bob's head, and his perspective on the game was changed from that day forth. Indeed, what is accomplished by a mad hack? If anything at all, it's still on the south side of nothing.

That's what makes the beginnings so precious—the chance to redeem all that has come before, to make a fresh start. Were you a complete boob on the last hole? You are not when you start the next hole. Now you're a champion again!

No other sport has had as much written about it as golf has, or by more distinguished authors: among others, John Updike, Herb Warren Wind, Mark Twain, and Winston Churchill. No other sport can pair a 90-year-old man with a 7-year-old girl and have them play with parity. No other sport asks participants to call penalties on themselves or to play their own foul balls.

> No other sport asks participants to call penalties on themselves or to play their own foul balls.

Another sage pointed out that people don't travel thousands of miles to play old tennis courts. But they will go halfway around the world to play golf in Scotland, Australia, or Hawaii. The opportunity to play a new course is as powerful a lure as there is in the world of sports, and we dream of the experience for months in advance.

Presidents, royals, rock stars, actors, and common folks all meet on this ancient playing field. How beautiful is that? You can pay $5 and play all day at some courses, or you can pay $50,000 and join a country club. It's your choice.

Even environmentalists have calmed their fury at golf. The chemicals found on a golf course these days are safer by far than those found on most lawns. Ask the birds, the deer, and the other critters who live on golf courses if they'd rather see a housing tract or a golf course. Audubon International has a certification program for golf courses, and many courses are following their prescription.

I've been lucky enough to play some of the best golf courses in the world: Augusta National, the Old Course at St. Andrews, Cypress Point, and Pebble Beach among them. To me, the Alister MacKenzie course at Cypress Point is the best of the lot, followed closely by (in order) St. Andrews, Pebble Beach, and Augusta National.

All of which is to say, you can go halfway around the world to play new courses, even as others are coming from halfway round the world to play in your backyard. Makes me feel like singing, "Will the circle be unbroken? By and by, Lord, by and by . . ." And while we're at it, we can think of golf as a circle, because as we finish one hole we begin the next. In my end is my beginning. The Buddha smiles.

Any Way You Slice It, Golf Is a Beautiful Game

Golf is a game for nuts and obsessives. It's played in almost every country on Earth, and it's even been played in space. Alan Shepard didn't take a baseball or soccer ball to the moon; he took a 6 iron. Some folks will do anything to get a little extra distance on a drive!

The late actor Jack Lemmon once said he would rather make the cut at the Crosby Clambake (more recently known as the AT&T Pebble Beach National Pro-Am) than win another Oscar. In the Philippines, then-president Ferdinand Marcos was notorious for letting nothing stand in the way of a round of golf—even enormous threat to life and limb. A midsize army of his secret service agents would surround the late president with oversize golf umbrellas as he set up for a shot—a position far too stationary for safety's sake—in order to shield him from the view of snipers. Another contingent of bodyguards would be stationed in the hills and bushes around the course, keeping watch for potential assassins.

Whether you are Zeppo Marx, Bing Crosby, Catherine Zeta-Jones, Bill Clinton, or Joe Smith, golf makes us all kindred spirits under the glove. I may not agree with your politics, but I can admire your skill with a wedge.

In the 6th century BC, the Greek philosopher Heraclitus declared, "A man's character is his fate." Twenty-five centuries later, noted golf writer Grantland Rice said, "Golf gives you an insight into human nature, your own as well as your opponent's. Eighteen holes of match or medal play will teach you more about your foe than will 18 years of dealing with him across a desk."

Both quotes say the same thing. Heraclitus might well have said, "A man's golf game is his fate," if only the Greeks had had the good sense to invent the game. (Of course if they had, it would now be an Olympic sport, maybe taking the place of something really exciting like curling or skeet shooting.) Play the game and your true character shows through. Would you do business with a man who throws his clubs or lies about his score?

We can all relate to that guy, though. As with windsurfing, where falling down 800 times is prerequisite to the 4.1 seconds of precarious balance the beginner eventually achieves, golf is not the easiest sport to master. Although novices don't fall in the water when learning to golf, there are plenty of times when they feel like tossing their Pings into a lake and jumping in after them. Learning golf is not graceful and should be done in private if at all possible. Personally, I'll do anything to avoid looking stupid in public, and though I have yet to fully master that art, at least when I'm on a golf course I'm around other people with the same affliction.

> Personally, I'll do anything to avoid looking stupid in public, . . . at least when I'm on a golf course I'm around other people with the same affliction.

I first embraced the game many years ago while living in Honolulu. You could find me daily practicing my putting and wedge shots in my living room. This presented some danger as I was living on the 14th floor of an apartment building and one errant chip could have ended up down by the pool. That was the extent to which I'd been bitten by the golf bug—I was willing to risk the embarrassment of having to go down and retrieve my ball from amongst the sunbathers and swimmers, not to mention the pieces of my window.

But that potential embarrassment was nothing compared with learning the game on actual golf courses. That, as you well know, is a lesson in humble pie. I pity the poor players who agreed to go a round with me in those early days. It's not that I didn't warn them—I let them know right up front that I was horrid.

"You couldn't be that bad," they would say at first, thinking I was trying to sandbag them. Then, after a few holes of proof, other sentiments ("Well, everybody has to learn") would emerge from between their clenched teeth. After a few more holes, a strange silence would come over the group, or they would stray off to talk about the finer points of the game with each other.

My chum Chris was a member at Waialae Country Club, where the Sony Open is played, and we'd go out there regularly. The 1st hole at Waialae is bordered on the right by some of the most expensive condominiums in Hawaii, in an area called Kahala Beach. Now, I'm right-handed and had a pretty wicked slice to my drive—need I say more? Luckily, golf carts can leave the scene pretty fast.

Chris was the kind of golfing partner who was kind enough to give me tips on my game. "Try softball," was one of his more germane comments. When he realized that I was going to persist, his advice was more to the point: "You're swinging way too hard. Your weight shift is far too exaggerated. Your arm and leg motion is too loose. Keep your head still; keep your eye on the ball. Don't pull back with your lead shoulder. Stop at the top of your backswing. Get your arms lower. You're chopping at the ball." All of which was great advice. The problem is, I'd step up to the ball with a head swimming in advice and produce a swing that made me look a lot like Frankenstein's monster on LSD.

More often than not, my ball would end up in the middle of the fairway—the wrong fairway. To that end, I started playing with yellow or orange balls to make sure I was picking up the right one. That, too, is a supreme embarrassment—having to pick up your yellow ball from the wrong fairway while real golfers are playing in the opposite direction. Colored balls are a sure sign of rank amateurism. Have you ever seen a pro use one?

Still, even when learning, golf is a nice walk in a grassy field. It's a game where boys are still allowed to be boys—and so are girls. After a good round, it is the best game ever invented; after a miserable round, the stupidest. In either case, see you tomorrow. Same time, same place.

The Patron Saint of Forgiveness: Seeking the Elusive Mulligan

Quick, give me the most familiar name in golf. Hogan? Woods? Nicklaus? Palmer?

May I suggest Mulligan? It's a name invoked by most golfers during most games. But who has any clue whatsoever as to the identity of this mysterious patron saint of forgiveness? Well, don't feel alone. Neither does the person walking down the fairway next to you. Nor, for that matter, do most golf historians. Nor, I readily admit, did I.

The glossary of the late Peter Dobereiner's *Golf Rules Explained* seemed a logical place to start searching for answers. Dobereiner described the Mulligan as the "practice, quite unofficial, of allowing a player a 'free' second drive when his first shot is unsatisfactory." Period, close quote. Nothing more? I mused.

So I consulted *The Historical Dictionary of Golfing Terms: From 1500 to Present* by Peter Davies. This book tells us that the origin of the term is "obscure" and quotes a 1960 Rex Lardner passage: "I don't even know if there was a Mulligan. But he gave his name to a wonderful gesture—letting you play a bad first drive over and no penalty."

Legendary golf professional Tommy Armour, less amused than Lardner by the concept of a do-over, was quoted in 1959 as saying, "When I first learned of a Mulligan in American golf I was astonished." Still, nothing on the origin of the term.

My real clue that the subject matter would be a deepwater dive came when I queried the late guru of golf writers, Dick Taylor. "Mulligan?" he asked perplexedly. "Obscure. I'll ask around." He did—with no luck. I figured that if Taylor was stumped, I was into the murky stuff of golf.

My dictionary lists only *Mulligan stew*, an Irish beef concoction that doesn't seem to have much to do with golf (even though beefing on a golf course is an integral part of the game), and *Gerry Mulligan*, the great jazz musician who also has no connection to golf. Several Web sites proclaim that our patron saint was in fact a certain David Mulligan of Montreal, Canada. From what I gathered, Mr. Mulligan had the task of driving his foursome to St. Lambert Country Club in the 1920s, and since he had to wrestle the steering wheel over rough road, his fellow players allowed him an extra drive on the 1st tee. A fair trade for gas money, I suppose.

In the late 1930s, Mulligan moved to the United States with the Biltmore Hotel chain and joined prestigious Winged Foot Golf Club in Mamaroneck, New York. The move improved his social status but not his drive from the 1st tee. He was a decent player, apparently, but he could never get off the 1st hole at his new course either, so the sporting members of Winged Foot—as did those at St. Lambert—gave him a free second ball.

> Mr. Mulligan had the task of driving his foursome to St. Lambert Country Club in the 1920s, and since he had to wrestle the steering wheel over rough road, his fellow players allowed him an extra drive on the 1st tee.

According to the book *Winged Foot Story: the Golf, the People, the Friendly Trees*, by Douglas LaRue Smith, "An early member of Winged Foot was one David Mulligan, a gentleman in the hotel business who came to us from Canada in 1937, when he joined Winged Foot and became president of New York's famous Biltmore Hotel. He is described as a friendly soul and raconteur who loved to tell his life's experiences while sitting in the upper locker room lounge. When he came to Winged Foot, legend has it that he would join a favorite foursome, not always the same, but usually made up of cronies in that prewar era who loved life and golf and their young club.

"Mulligan played a fair game, but he was, as they say, a slow starter. His drive off the 1st tee oft went astray. Turning plaintively to his friends he would plead, or perhaps only look, saying 'Another?' Being generous souls they would nod, permissively, if not enthusiastically. David is remembered by our senior members today for his warmth, and the pleasure he had while sitting in the lounge with his Scotch and soda, proudly claiming credit for golf's most generous gesture, the Mulligan."

The Royal & Ancient may respond to this much as the Ayatollah Khomeini responded to Salman Rushdie's *The Satanic Verses*—that is, as blasphemy. In fact, even Winged Foot adds a disclaimer at the bottom of the story, noting, "We should say that the Mulligan has never been accepted by serious golfers as legitimate. Some who tolerate it passively insist that if the second shot is taken, it must be played. A larger number may take their choice of the two [sometimes called a Finnegan], but at Winged Foot as at many fine golf courses, and among the Scots, it is frowned on if not discouraged altogether."

So there you have it—mystery solved. Personally, I feel quite justified in invoking the name of such a generous and nonserious (at least not overly so) golfing soul at the 1st tee, and perhaps occasionally the 2nd. Well, once in a while on the 3rd. OK, let's be honest here—never past the 18th.

While the practice may not merit a Nobel Peace Prize, all golfers should at least raise a toast (preferably Scotch and soda) to the immortal David Mulligan. And if you happen to spill the first one all over your shirt, don't worry. Dave would be most happy if you just tried it again.

Couples Golf

Ladies, I'm going to have to ask you to stop reading here and please skip to the next chapter. You see, the following discussion reveals certain trade secrets of the male species, as well as observations and advice for his eyes only. Thank you, and I'll see you in a few pages.

Gentlemen, here are a few things I've discovered about couples golf. First, if you *do* want your spouse or significant other to join you on the golf course, definitely don't invite her. At least that's the way it worked in my household. My wife, Landry, was one of those people who thought golf was just about the silliest thing a person could do in life—until she met me. Then her thinking changed. All of a sudden golf was not just silly; it was also her competition for my time on weekends. So she took up the game.

> First, if you *do* want your spouse or significant other to join you on the golf course, definitely don't invite her.

For my part, I didn't invite, push, pull, woo, or rebuff. I just went along merrily, doing what I always do, which is play once or twice a week. I never said, "C'mon, honey, pretty please, come with me." Nor did I say, "You know what, women are not all that welcome at the golf course anyway" (which would surely have gotten her redheaded dander up!). No, every Friday I just mentioned casually that I had a Sunday morning tee time, bright and early. That really got to her, and soon she started suggesting that she was free then, too.

On the other hand, if you really *don't* want your spouse to play, make a point of begging her to do so. A little *reverse psychology* always helps in a relationship, right? If it turns out that you are as lucky as I am, and your better half does take up the game— love you, hon!—there are a few other things to remember. For example, never give her instruction of any kind. This is a surefire recipe for disaster. I tried, but with my sweet and understanding Landry—love you, hon!—this was akin to using logic to win an argument. It just doesn't work.

I valiantly suggested for several years that maybe she should aim farther left, since she consistently hit her tee shot into the right rough or behind the trees to that side. "No, I always hit it straight," she'd insist. So one day I charted her tee shots: right, right, right, right, right. You get the picture. But that didn't make *me* right. "Now I'm hitting right because you're watching," she said. You put the thought in my mind. What do you expect?" Uh, um, uh—love you, hon! As soon as she was told by a noted instructor, however, that her tendency was to aim right when she set up, she immediately accepted the information and corrected the problem.

Which brings me to another point: Never say anything like, "But sweetums, haven't I been telling you that exact same thing for the last 5 years?" That, my friend, was a direct challenge to my redhead (and probably would be to any other head you might be in a relationship with). Now when we play, she'll set up for her shot, look at me for approval of her alignment, and, if she still hits it to the right, put the blame squarely on me. "What happened?" she'll ask, perturbed. "I thought you said I was lined up properly."

Which brings me to point number whatever: You cannot win, my friend. No matter what. In this regard, golf reflects life, in which you are swimming upstream when disagreeing with your mate. In the grand scheme of things, I figure Landry and I are pretty fortunate. Once I learned my role and my lines, things started going very smoothly for us. Besides, we play together only a couple of times per month.

I often ponder, though, what might have transpired if I had been a true Golf Nut—capital G, capital N. There are such people, and they belong to a group called the Golf Nut Society. Their goal is to play as often as they can—as many holes per day—come hell or high water, personal injury, or hurt feelings. In fact, if they could somehow combine all those calamities into a single day and play through them, the society would hold them aloft as royalty.

When a member does indeed go above and beyond—which of course is their goal—he will find himself in the running for Golf Nut of the Year (GNOY), a high honor that many strive to achieve but only one extra-diligent person is able to accomplish annually. A recent article in the *Los Angeles Times* pointed out that Michael Jordan won the coveted GNOY title in 1989 after he skipped the ceremony awarding him the NBA Most Valuable Player trophy to get in 36 holes in Pinehurst, N.C. Gentlemen, if you think you have a shot at the glory afforded by being GNOY—and for fair warning, there are some 4,000 other souls vying—you can take the "How nuts are you?" entrance exam and see where you rank in national golf zaniness.

Which brings me to my final piece of advice: No matter how nuts you are about the game, your spouse, girlfriend, or other mate (your dog excluded) is not likely to share your gusto. Therefore, put your local florist on speed dial. And remember—no matter what happens out there on the links, it's just not worth arguing over. But if you do run afoul of your significant other, order flowers and use the three little words that always make everything better: "Love you, hon!"

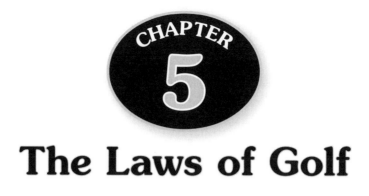

The Laws of Golf

Ever noticed how the best round of your life is invariably followed by the worst? How that amazing birdie is always followed by a double bogey? How the only putt you sink all day is the one you don't care about and don't try on? How you just can't stand prosperity?

Don't despair. You are not alone; golfers the world over share the same fate. And although it doesn't help to know them—since in this case knowledge does not equate to power—golf is governed by certain inalienable tenets: the Laws of Golf (not to be confused with the *Rules of Golf* as issued by the United States Golf Association or the Royal & Ancient).

Numerous versions of the Laws of Golf have circulated via the World Wide Web in recent years, and most of them are factually incorrect. I have included here what I believe to be the original 25 laws, thought to have been written by Old Tom Morris

> You are not alone; golfers the world over share the same fate.

(1821–1908) in 1860 in anticipation of the very first Open Championship (which we in the States—offensively to most Brits, who consider it the only worthy championship—now refer to as the British Open).

The claim that these were the original 25 laws is substantiated by the fact that a handwritten version of these exact words was purchased by an unwitting Scot at a garage sale in St. Andrews in 2005. Experts have verified the handwriting as that of Old Tom Morris.

LAW 1

Your best round of golf will be followed almost immediately by your worst round ever. The probability of the latter increases with the number of people you tell about the former.

LAW 2

A good warm-up session on the driving range always spells trouble on the golf course. The better the warm-up, the worse the round.

LAW 3

Brand new golf balls are drawn to water. Though this cannot be proven in the lab, it is a known fact that the more expensive the golf ball, the greater its attraction to water.

LAW 4

Golf balls never bounce off of trees and back into play. If one does, the tree is breaking a Law of Golf and should be cut down.

LAW 5

No matter what causes a golfer to muff a shot, all playing partners must solemnly chant, "You looked up," or "Not your best shot," or something equally infuriating.

LAW 6

The higher a golfer's handicap, the more qualified he deems himself as an instructor.

LAW 7

Every par 3 hole in the world has a secret desire to humiliate golfers, and the shorter the hole, the greater its desire.

LAW 8

A golfer hitting into your group will always be bigger than anyone in your group. Likewise, if you accidentally hit into a group, it will consist of a football player, a professional wrestler, a convicted murderer, and a lawyer.

LAW 9

Golf balls from the same sleeve tend to follow one another, particularly out of bounds or into the water (see law 3).

LAW 10

The person you would most hate to lose to will always be the one who beats you.

LAW 11

The last three holes of a round will automatically adjust your score to what it really should be.

LAW 12

When you walk up to your ball on the putting surface, it's invariably 2 inches or less from where yesterday's hole was cut.

LAW 13

All vows taken on a golf course shall be valid only until sunset.

LAW 14

Since bad shots come in groups of three, your fourth consecutive bad shot is really the beginning of the next group of three.

LAW 15

When you look up and cause an awful shot, you will always look down again at exactly the moment when you should have continued watching the ball if you ever wanted to see it again.

LAW 16

Golfers who claim they don't cheat also lie.

LAW 17

A golf match is a test of your skill against your opponent's luck.

LAW 18

It's surprisingly easy to hole a 50-foot putt when you lie 8 and don't care anymore.

LAW 19

Counting on your opponent to inform you when he breaks a rule is like expecting him to make fun of his own haircut.

LAW 20

Nonchalant putts count the same as chalant putts.

LAW 21

You can hit a 2-acre fairway 10 percent of the time and a 2-inch branch 90 percent of the time.

LAW 22

Every time a golfer makes a birdie, he or she must subsequently make two triple bogeys to restore the fundamental equilibrium of the universe.

LAW 23

There are two things you can learn by stopping your backswing at the top and checking the position of your hands: how many hands you have and which one is wearing the glove.

LAW 24

Any ball you can see in the rough from 50 yards away is not yours.

LAW 25

Any club that feels "absolutely perfect" in the shop has no chance whatsoever of performing well on the golf course. In other words, don't buy a driver until you've had a chance to throw it.

CHAPTER 6

Forget Love—
Laugh at the One
You're With

One of the most common responses people give when asked what they love most about their spouse or significant other is that he or she makes them laugh. The same is true about golf: One of the things we love about the game is its ability to make us laugh.

Of course, that's quite a challenge when you've just missed a 3-foot birdie putt and helicoptered your putter into the branches of a tree. But just as when we argue with our loved ones, we need to remember the many things we love about the game, issue a quick curse under our breath, smile, and move on. There are, after all, 17 more holes to play.

When it's funny, there's no better game in the world. I for one have literally fallen out of golf carts from laughing so hard, as I did the time my pal Jimbo Pivarnik was trying desperately to hit a 5 wood in the 13th fairway at Mauna Kea Golf Course on the Big Island of Hawaii. One . . . two . . . three . . . four desperate hacks, with the ball moving only a few feet forward each time. Finally, with a big huff, Jimbo spanked it soundly—straight into the bushes on the right. Now that was funny, at least to me.

I laughed myself out of breath watching Gary Terlecki, a guy I had just met on the 1st tee, do the boogaloo and the funky chicken to try to get his putt moving in the direction of the hole.

"Don't hurt yourself," I finally managed to say, but Gary didn't care. He was in a world of his own.

I nearly split my sides when Andy Olstein, a fellow golf writer, hit the ball so hard—and so sideways—that it took a 3-inch chip out of the concrete tee marker before careening wildly somewhere we never discovered. While I was laughing, Andy stormed off the course in anger. After he was gone, I picked up the damaged tee marker, and over dinner that night I had our waiter bring it out and serve it to him on a silver platter. He finally saw the humor.

I stood in shock and awe as Brett McMullen swung his 3 wood so forcefully that it snapped in half and wilted in his hand like a dead flower. I couldn't believe my eyes when Tim Bradley's 40-foot putt rolled past the cup by a full 2 feet and was then blown backward by the Christmas morning winds right into the hole. Those are the moments that make golf a fun game. Sure, I'll take the occasional great shot, but they're rare. Golf is a game I like best when it's fun.

> Sure, I'll take the occasional great shot, but they're rare. Golf is a game I like best when it's fun.

Then there are those other moments when my friends have a chance to laugh at me. Like most golfers, I'm highly creative when it comes to my game, and not only with a pencil, though like everyone I've taken my share of "courtesy doubles" and "gimme" putts—from 6 feet away.

My greatest act of creativity is in the thinking process that allows me to continue on in the face of humiliation and despair. My logic allows me to change gloves, balls, shirts—anything to achieve that perfect harmony with the stars, the exact crossing of power points which will propel my game back to its normal mediocrity and out of a lifelong slump.

One must appreciate people who make the game fun. Each year at the AT&T Pebble Beach National Pro-Am, comedian and actor Bill Murray makes us all smile. The Three Stooges had a classic golf routine, too, which played out in their 1935 film *Three Little Beers*, wherein the fictitious Panther Brewing Company excludes its three new delivery men (the Stooges) from its annual golf tournament. The Stooges get really teed off and come up with a plan to gain entry, with an eye on winning the $100 first prize. Too bad they're as bad at golf as they are at delivering beer. I still crack up at the thought of Moe smacking Larry or Curly on top of the noggin with a club.

Even Jed Clampett had his round on the golf course. In a classic *Beverly Hillbillies* episode, Jed and Jethro are invited to "shoot some golfs" with bank president Mr. Drysdale, who takes the additional step of sending over some equipment. Thinking that "shooting golfs" is something akin to shooting raccoons, Jed and Jethro are excited, seeing as how they haven't been hunting since they were poor mountaineers, barely keeping their family fed.

Inspecting the clubs and shoes that Drysdale sends over, Jed, who is quite enthused, says, "Them golfs must be some tough critters. First you shoot 'em, then you club 'em, then you spike 'em. For pure scrappiness, they make a mountain lion look like a pussycat!" Hail to Uncle Jed and all the comics and sages on golf courses. They keep the game fun, and it should be fun. That is a lesson we all need to relearn frequently.

PART

II

The Power
Game

Desperately Seeking 3 Wood

To some guys, all the hi-tech equipment talk makes perfect sense. They will understand if you tell them a driver imparts an "extremely high eMOI that exceeds 5800 (USGA conforming)," a shaft has a "3.5-degree torque and a .350 tip size," or a set of irons boasts "minimal offset and higher CG position [to] enhance the player's ability to work the ball left, right, high, and low for increased control and accuracy." Huh?

When I'm car shopping, I'm not at all interested in knowing the technical workings of my new shock absorbers; I just want to know if the ride is smooth. Likewise, I don't want to enroll in an MIT advanced engineering class to understand how my golf clubs work or how the principles of coefficient drag and aero-dynamic dimples affect the flight of the golf ball. I just want the damn thing to go in the hole.

Early on in golf's long and murky history, equipment selection was simple. You had a tree branch in your hand and a rock at your foot, so you decided to while away the day seeing if you could roll the rock into yonder ground furrow as the sheep were grazing nearby. Gee, sounds like a lot of fun.

But from there, things got complicated—and expensive—pretty fast. You wouldn't want to be the only bloke in town still hitting those stupid rocks when old Allan Robertson, one of the first professional golfers and equipment makers in St. Andrews, was carving wood into rounded orbs and calling them "golf balls," would you?

Then, before you could beg, borrow, or steal enough quid to pay Allan, someone somewhere decided to stuff boiled goose feathers into cowhide pouches, sew them up tight, and hit them around the pasture instead. Sure, it didn't hurt quite so much as rock or wood, but c'mon—what about tradition? Besides, rocks are free.

Nowadays, golfers are faced with a vast array of equipment choices. Dozens of companies manufacture dozens of products, and each claims to be the absolute best. How can we tell them apart?

We have woods made of metal; clubs crafted of space-age composites; and balls designed with materials you've never heard of (what is "surlyn," anyway?) to fly higher, straighter, and farther and to stop faster. We're given exact data via GPS satellite technology regarding precisely how far it is to every hole on every golf course in the world, yet my ball still won't go in. But isn't that what I was promised when I paid my $300? Am I the only one who is confused by all this?

The truth is that for many years I've been desperately seeking a 3 wood that I could count on. Some people swear by their 3 woods; I swear *at* mine. I've sampled plenty in the store (where they always seem to work just fine), proceeded to spend a small fortune, gone to the course thinking I'd finally solved my 3 wood dilemma, and not hit one damn ball straight.

> We're given exact data via GPS satellite technology regarding precisely how far it is to every hole on every golf course in the world, yet my ball still won't go in.

Now when I read the glossy magazine ads or stand in the store aisle, I'm caught between believing the manufacturer's hype and thinking to myself, "No, it's all sizzle and no steak." What manufacturer does *not* claim that its club is better than all others, and that because of this or that brilliant new advance in research and design all my problems on the golf course will be solved? Then they launch into a blaze of techno-babble. Huh?

Recently I ran across a club from Pinemeadow Golf called the DoubleWall Fairway Wood. I'd never heard of the brand, but the claim was alluring: "The DoubleWall has been independently tested to have the 'Biggest Sweet Spot' in golf. It is engineered with a patented inner wall inside the club head that dramatically improves performance. This revolutionary new technology creates an extraordinarily strong power chamber improving performance over the entire hitting surface of the club."*

Huh?

A little farther down the 3 wood aisle, Nickent trumpets its innovation in thinning "the face of the 3DX DC, creating a much higher C.O.R. than the original 3DX Ironwood. A special plasma welding process was used to help redistribute the weight to the extreme perimeters of the clubhead."**

Double-huh?

The more I hear, the more confusing buying a 3 wood becomes. Just once, I want to read where a manufacturer admits something like this: "TaylorMade's club is better than ours, hands down. They spent the money; they did the research. Look no further." I'd probably buy that guy's club just to reward his honesty!

But nooooo. Everyone thinks theirs is the better widget. Nike, TaylorMade, Callaway, or whoever—the message is largely the same from every manufacturer: "Buy mine, buy mine. I have the solution. This is the last $300 you'll ever have to spend on a 3 wood." Then more words like "extremely high eMOI," and all I hear is "blah, blah, blah."

Unfortunately for me, I'm still helicoptering one 3 wood after another into the tree branches of my home course. My game is not improving—and you can bet it has cost me a pretty penny— but I sure am making a lovely piece of modern art.

* Source: Pinemeadow Golf, www.pinemeadowgolf.com
** Source: Nickent Golf, www.nickentgolf.com

CHAPTER
8

Making Fast Friends
on the Links

Being children of the New World disallows us from giving our golfing clubs such lofty, powerful names as Royal and Ancient Golf Club of St Andrews, the Honourable Company of Edinburgh Golfers, or the Gentlemen Golfers of Leith, as clubs in Scotland are historically wont to do. Yet the golfing clubs of America account for a large part of the 26 million golfers in this country.

Personally, I've been a member of three clubs over the years: the Penmar-by-the-Sea Type-Os, where I currently pay dues; the Hard Drivers of Honolulu (hardly a distinguished name, yet appropriate for its computer-oriented, golf-nutty members whose main thrill was trying to hit the ball a million miles); and the Royal and Recent Golf Club of Hilton Head. This latter motley crew was made up mostly of writers and magazine people but also included some other sporting men and women with whom I enjoyed association. We totaled 20 members.

We were not all great golfers, but we all hit the ball hard. The old adage "the woods are full of power hitters" applied to most of us, but hey—they didn't pay to watch Babe Ruth bunt. Our handicaps ranged from 1.7 to 40, but when we got together, handicaps mattered not in the least. Our primary function as a club was to gather, enjoy a day on the links, and then gather again in the early evening for a feast that was often dubbed "Dueling Lasagna" or some such thing, wherein six or seven brave souls volunteered to cook the same dish using their own tried-and-true recipes.

After we consumed far too much lasagna, or whatever the dish might be—plus the salads, wines (and vodka, scotch, beer . . . you get the idea), breads, and desserts—the bragging, laughing, and loud pronouncements would invariably ensue. These were followed by louder pronouncements, often regarding the day's games: who beat the skunk out of whom, who would get revenge next time out, and so on, and it rarely stopped there.

> Our primary function as a club was to gather, enjoy a day on the links, and then gather again in the early evening for a feast that was often dubbed "Dueling Lasagna" or some such thing.

As clear as yesterday, I recall one three-sheets-to-the-wind golfer who became so eloquent one evening that he stood on a chair at the head of our long table and began excitedly slurring verses from the Russian poet Vladimir Mayakovsky, which somehow explained why he couldn't sink a putt that afternoon on the golf course. Sadly, we all understood exactly what he meant.

At the end of the evening, those who could still manage to stand and walk were herded into a judging group to vote on who had produced the "Best Lasagna," whose dish was the "Most Original," who was "Most Likely Not to Be Invited to Cook Again," and so forth. It was all great fun. Then we'd hand out the day's prizes: "Closest to the Pin," "Closest to the Alligators," "Most Lost Balls," "Most Ineffective Partner" (there were always quite a few nominations in this category), "Most Creative Use of the Golf Course," and "Biggest Sandbagger."

Our by-now-weaving tournament chair—usually me—would then publicly avow to never allow such a mockery of the great and holy sport to occur again, after which we'd plan our next outing, hoping the exact same thing would happen.

I've heard stories about this ritual being carried out by various golf clubs and in differing forms from coast to coast and around the globe. After all is said and done about the great golf courses of the world, the amazing achievements of the touring professionals, the technological advances in the equipment industry, and everything else we talk about, the one thing that keeps golf afloat is the desire of us common people to play together in the grassy fields under the warming sun, to share the triumphs and tribulations of our collective obsession, and then to eat and drink way too much.

Whether or not the members of the group know each other well when the day begins, they will likely be fast friends by the time the sun sets—or, in extreme cases, rises again the next morning (such as when the guys went on a golfing holiday to Myrtle Beach, but that's a story I promised never to write!).

America's golf clubs form the backbone of the game in this country. Though the U.S. Open is contested over some of our nation's more private and prestigious club courses—such as Shinnecock Hills Golf Club, Oakmont Country Club, Oakland Hills Country Club—just about every municipal and public course has its men's and women's clubs comprised of regular sandbaggers and hackers like you and me. Many hold weekend tournaments, and all offer a method to submit scores for calculating handicaps. But that's not really the point.

Be it public, private, corporate golf, client golf, or a weekend club just going to visit Dr. Green, it all amounts to the same thing: people getting together in a spirit of relaxation and camaraderie to make fast and lasting friends on the links and to eat and sometimes drink too much afterward. That's the joy of it all. My one piece of advice is this: Don't partner with the guy quoting Mayakovsky poems—he can't putt.

CHAPTER 9

Hype Versus Reality—
Can You Believe This?

"It's the Augusta National of Texas," a golf course architect recently remarked to me as we waited to tee off on his latest masterpiece in the heart of the Lone Star State. Since we were standing in the middle of a vast, arid, treeless plain, I thought he was joking, so I countered, "No, it's not. There's not a tree or hill in sight—certainly no brilliant azaleas." "But that's how they want to talk about themselves," the architect persisted.

Architects are power guys in the game, so I was surprised this one was biting the spin apple so hard. We're deluged with hype every day in magazines and newspapers, blitzed on television, and squawked at by the radio. Highway billboards, Web site banners, the sides of buses, e-mail spam . . . Where does it end? The pressure to spin everything in our society even causes sane men like Jack Nicklaus, Tom Fazio, and others to describe their newest design efforts with phrases like "This could just be the best piece of land I've ever had to work with." Emphasis on "could be."

I remember attending a new course opening near Hilton Head Island several years ago. Part of the course fronted marshland, and part ran through scrawny pine, but never mind that. The well-respected course designer described it as "the Pebble Beach of South Carolina." There must be a "Pebble Beach" for every state in the union. I've lost count of the number of times I've played "the best finishing holes in golf," "the best stretch of holes on earth," or "the most photographed hole in the world." So many make the same claims!

There must be a "Pebble Beach" for every state in the union.

How about this favorite of course designers: "God did the design; I just planted the grass." Sure, and did God bury that elephant on the 16th green? And here's a snippet of nonsense that writers and public relations people like to use: "Challenging yet playable for all levels of golfers." I get that one in my e-mail several times a week about various courses. What does it mean?

"Championship golf course" is a phrase I see describing courses all the time, generally ones that have never held more than a club championship, won by the guys with the best sandbags. That's like a brand-spanking-new tournament on the PGA Tour calling itself a "Classic," as in "The South Podunk Classic." The spin itself is about the only thing that's classic about these tournaments, at least for the next 25 years or so. As my friend and fellow golf writer Chris Duthie reminds me, "The spin machine has never met a hyperbole it couldn't overstate."

I've used hype-speak myself, so I know how tempting it is, but in the end, my vote is for truth in advertising. So I'm fessing up. Here are some of my favorite hype phrases, conveniently translated for you into plain-speak:

- "A couple of questionable holes" means "I scored a triple bogey here."
- "For all levels of golfers" means "It's not a very challenging course."
- "Wide fairways" means "You'd have to doink a ducky to miss this fairway."
- "Tight fairways" means "What was this designer possibly thinking?"
- "An ambitious development" means "It'll never fly."

- "The 'other' course on the property is . . ." means "The other course is the weak sister."
- "Some holes play farther than you think" means "I dumped one into the arroyo."
- "Avoid the bunkers" means "My game stinks."
- "Well-placed bunkers" means "If the course designer's car was in the parking lot, I'd slash his tires."
- "This course doesn't live up to its reputation" means "They didn't give me a free golf shirt."
- "The back nine has a completely different personality" means "I had a couple beers at the turn and I can't remember the home holes for the life of me."
- "Don't lose your concentration on this scenic hole" means "I couldn't think of anything else to say."
- "Challenging yet playable" means "This course isn't all that good, but I needed the money so I wrote the story."

Designers and architects might need a little truth in advertising, too:

- "This is a magnificent piece of property" means "I'm under contract to make glowing, meaningless statements about the course."
- "Club selection is important" means "I've got you by the tighty whities here."
- "Easy bogey, tough par" means "I own your 26-handicap rear end."
- "The greens have some subtle movement" means "You ain't sinkin' a putt all day."
- "The two most striking features are the trees and the stream" means "Ho-hum . . . oh, is the microphone on?"
- "God did the design" means "Better write nice things or you're going to hell."

Instead, I'd just love to hear some designer say this:

- "This place was basically flat and barren; it's a wonder anything grows out here."
- "It requires pinpoint accuracy off the tee—something not even I can do."
- "I did the best I could (with this uninteresting patch of dirt)."
- "It's the St. Andrews of Kentucky."
- "Well, it ain't Pebble Beach or Augusta National."
- "I needed the money."

And from developers:

- "Nicklaus or Fazio would have done better, but we couldn't afford those guys."
- "Hey, it's a real estate development; where would you have put the homes?"
- "We redefine hospitality: The course is just OK, but our booze is first-rate!"
- "We've reserved a limited number of tee times for public play each day; the county made us do it."
- "We're committed to the environment; otherwise, who'd buy out here?"
- "I'm thankful for the EPA's toxic waste clean-up program; otherwise I'd be unemployed and we'd all be knee deep in stank right now."
- "I needed the money."
- "Yes, there's a hotel and another golf course on the master plan, but just now we've spent all our money getting where we are."

So there you have it. Now don't go running back to my previous stories to find out what I really meant when I said all those fluffy things. You'll only get me in trouble. There are a great many courses to play, but truth be told, they are what they are—sometimes a great course, sometimes a great notion. If you'd like my advice: Avoid the bunkers, have a few beers at the turn, keep your concentration on the scenic holes, and remember, if all else fails, you are just *one* level of golfer.

CHAPTER 10

The Game of the Future? Let's Hope Not

I read an article the other day about a new championship golf course under construction in North Carolina that was being touted as "longer than 8,000 yards." C'mon, why not 10,000 yards? And while we're at it, can't we make those pesky holes an inch smaller? Why make the game so damn *easy?*

It used to be that a "championship" course in this country was around 6,000 yards long. No more. With advancements in equipment technology and an emphasis on strength training among the current generation of touring pros, some of those older courses just don't pose much of a challenge to today's best players.

Of course, the rest of us 26 million hack dogs might slip into catatonic depression if designers made their new courses more difficult to play.

> The main thing to consider when building a new course is that Tiger won't shoot 30 under par if he ever happens to show up.

But who cares? The main thing to consider when building a new course is that Tiger won't shoot 30 under par if he ever happens to show up.

All this got me thinking: What will the golf course of the future look like? How far will technology be allowed to push the game? What will the golf experience be in 5, 10, or 20 years? So I asked several well-respected pros and golf course architects these burning questions of our day. Since I did not hear back from anyone (I'm relieved that—unlike me—they are all too busy working to answer these kinds of ridiculous inquiries), here is a sampling of the ideas and predictions they might have come up with.

10,000-Yard Standard

Within 5 years, all new 18-hole courses will surpass 10,000 yards. The added length will be necessary because equipment currently being tested—we've heard rumors of a golf ball that produces a tiny nuclear reaction when struck and of hammer-headed drivers constructed with next-generation ballistic polyethylene fibers equipped with diamond-face inserts—will produce drives in excess of 400 yards by the average player. Duffers will feel like Superman, but courses will have to get longer, and 600-yard par 4s and 350-yard par 3s will be commonplace.

Six-Hole Courses

Concurrent with 10,000-yard courses—and the typical 7-hour rounds they will produce—a proliferation of six-hole courses will emerge, aimed at those among us who are too busy to devote an entire day to a round of golf. Catering to the hectic modern lifestyle of people who actually have to work for a living, the 6-hole loop will become the preferred style of play for many. "Get in, play fast, and get out" will be the USGA's new mantra, as they try anything and everything to increase the number of rounds played in the United States. It's even possible that someone will institute a program whereby a golfer has only to play one or two holes, after which a surrogate will step in to finish. "Aha!" you'll be able to announce when your pseudo-score is e-mailed to you during an important business meeting, "I just shot a 28 for six holes!"

Techno Golf Carts

Within 3 years, golf carts will come equipped with iPod plug-ins, built-in BlackBerrys, and flat screen televisions split-tuned to the Golf Channel and Fox News, since golfers tend to lean in those directions. Two years later, super techno-advanced carts will appear, complete with golf simulators that depict the course you are currently playing. Where these carts are in use, savvy businesspeople will never really have to step onto the grass at all, as a screen avatar will play the course for you (and a heck of a lot better than you could!).

12-Inch-Wide Holes

Within 10 years, slow play on 10,000-yard courses will get so bad that the USGA will mandate widening the cup. Britain's eminently quotable statesman Winston Churchill once quipped: "Golf is a game whose aim is to hit a very small ball into an even smaller hole, with weapons singularly ill-designed for the purpose." So let's make the dang hole bigger!

It was another Brit, Ben Wright (the CBS golf commentator who was unceremoniously shown stage left after he allegedly commented to a newspaper reporter that women were inhibited from playing truly great golf by certain frontal parts of their anatomy), who first suggested this out loud. Wright might have had Churchill's comment in mind when he decided that the ridiculously small size of the golf hole is the main reason for slow play.

> Winston Churchill once quipped: "Golf is a game whose aim is to hit a very small ball into an even smaller hole, with weapons singularly ill-designed for the purpose."

Currently 4.25 inches wide—as mandated in rules published in 1891 by the governing body of golf in Europe, the Royal and Ancient Golf Club of St Andrews—Wright postulated that a 12-inch-wide hole would speed play considerably. "It's difficult enough getting to the putting surface," he protested. "Why not make it easier to putt?" If and when the PGA Tour ever plays the course, reduce the hole circumference to 3 inches wide.

The Indoor Golf Course

Inclement weather can cost operators of golf courses big bucks. One day of rain equals thousands of dollars of lost revenue. Courses in snow country literally lose months of revenue each year. And the skills of golfers who are unable to play because of the bad weather grow rusty. These problems and others are resolved by way of the indoor golf course: Artificial turf, here we come. No more lost balls! Errant shots merely bounce off the wall and back toward the hole.

The potential global market is massive. In Japan, for example, where the game is wildly popular, most golfers have never been on an actual golf course. Three-tier driving ranges are popular in Japan, and the vast majority of the millions who use them play on them exclusively. Drop an indoor course on the top of a high rise, and the inhabitants would be one step closer to heaven.

Golf Leash

Within one year, some genius inventor will bring to market the Golf Leash. No more will your spouse or child throw clubs in frustration or anger. The Golf Leash straps those uncooperative clubs to the wrist via a patented bungee cord attachment, ensuring that the thrown club will immediately recoil at the thrower, often causing well-deserved bodily injury. How many times do you think they'll have to learn that lesson?

Golf Ear Plugs

I'm surprised no one has invented this one already, but within 6 months someone will. The promotional literature will read like this: Do you get annoyed every time your spouse or even a complete stranger gives you stupid "tips" on how to correct your swing? (And ever notice how the person giving the "tip" is usually a miserable golfer?) Imagine reaching into your golf bag and pulling out your one-size-fits-all Golf Ear Plugs and slipping them smugly—er, snugly—into your ears. You'll relish the silence! And the look on the face of your erstwhile "teacher" will be priceless. Guaranteed he or she won't make par the rest of the day.

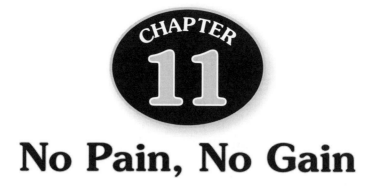

No Pain, No Gain

Sooner or later, every great athlete has to play through pain. We hear of golfers on the professional tours all the time who tee it up with wrist injuries, sore backs, bad shoulders, and—particularly as they get older—bad everything else. The same syndrome affects us less-than-great athletes. Despite the fact that those who don't play the game consider it a "noncontact" sport, golf is anything but that, especially for those who power up to win the long drive competition on every shot. And it takes its toll.

Think about it: We make contact with the ground on every swing, with clubhead speeds of up to 120 miles per hour. There's nothing "noncontact" about enacting that bone-jarring movement 90 or 100 times a day. But unlike Tiger Woods, who showed the world his superhuman side by amazingly winning the 2008 U.S. Open with a fractured fibula and a knee that required surgery, most of us mere mortals are unable to perform to the highest levels of our capabilities while injured.

Personally, I wither at the mere sight of my own blood and head straight for the clubhouse bar for a few toddies the instant my back so much as whispers "Ouch." Wuss? Maybe, but I'm a guy who sees no clear point in slogging on through sideways rain, mud, high winds, or triple bogeys. Add an injury to the mix and

I wither at the mere sight of my own blood and head straight for the clubhouse bar for a few toddies the instant my back so much as whispers "Ouch."

suddenly reruns of *Gilligan's Island* start to sound very appealing. Still, there have been a few times when it was impossible to slip away unnoticed or when hobbling off the course would have been too embarrassing . . . even for me.

A few years ago, for example, I was writing a guidebook to the golf courses of Hawaii and was in the midst of playing every course in the state for my research. (I know, tough duty. The sympathy cards keep coming to this day.) The book was to include reviews of the state's seven military courses, and in the course of my inquiries I headed one morning to Honolulu's Navy-Marine Golf Course. Naturally, military personnel play military courses, and wimps like me are less-than-enthusiastically tolerated.

By some random or playful stroke of fortune, I happened to get paired that day with two of the sternest-looking Marines I had ever seen. These guys made it clear from the outset that they didn't take kindly to a civilian—particularly a hippie, writer-type—invading their turf, and they reacted as if they had just been ordered into a combat zone. Corporal Butcher glaringly introduced himself to me on the first tee with a steely handshake, barked orders at his golf ball, and frowned like he was going to court-martial the ball when it disobeyed: "TURN!" "SIT!" "GET IN THE HOLE!" His voice was sharp and cadenced like that of a drill sergeant. Its intended effect: intimidation. The result? His golf ball was unfazed, but I was terrified.

His playing partner, PFC Slaughter, was equally stiff. Between them, I saw not so much as a smile the entire round. Indeed, if they relaxed a single muscle, it was undetectable to me. When it was my turn to hit, they'd glower at me as if I were an enemy fighter and they my hawkishly diligent foes. I can only surmise that these two soldiers could play through a great deal of pain.

Unfortunately for me, being the wuss that I am, what would have been an uncomfortable round became downright excruciating when I stupidly caught my left foot between my moving golf cart and the cart-path curb on hole 4. As the sign pasted on the windshield indicates, I can personally attest that dangling your limbs outside the cart while driving can be hazardous.

I muffled a scream, not wanting to appear any wimpier to my companions than they had already determined I was. Blood had already soaked through my white sock, and when I pulled the sock down below my ankle I could see where my skin had been torn away by the concrete. Then my leg started to throb up to my knee. I started thinking about how I could escape to *Gilligan's Island* reruns and booze-heavy toddies.

But when I looked up at Butcher and Slaughter—their real names, I kid you not—they were staring at me, both expressionless. Without acknowledging my mishap, nor so much as asking, "Are you OK?" Butcher glanced at my bloody ankle, then motioned to the tee with his head as if to say, "What? You're up, wuss. Hit the ball."

I limped to the tee box, blood now leaking out of my sock and onto my shoe. Somehow, I managed to hit the tee shot, putting my weight on my right leg. The two Marines were dead silent. They watched me limp back to my cart and followed me down the fairway. They stayed on my tail for the rest of the day, watching closely, as if to say, "YOU WANNA PLAY OUT HERE? THIS IS A MARINE BASE, BOY. WE DON'T CARE IF YOU'RE BLEEDING!" Any thought I had of escape was thus dashed by these two fine United States Marines.

Golfers injuring themselves while playing—or dangling their limbs out of golf carts—is bad enough, but sometimes it's dangerous to even be a spectator at a golf tournament. Former President Gerald Ford, for instance, was famous for beaning people in the gallery, and once in a while the celebrities he shared carts with had to duck, too. "He barely missed me a couple times," Arnold Palmer once joked in an interview with the Associated Press.

Luckily, Ford saw the humor of it all. "Back on my home course in Grand Rapids, Michigan," he told a dinner gathering at the World Golf Hall of Fame in 1974, "they don't yell 'Fore!' they yell 'Ford!'" Bob Hope, with whom Mr. Ford shared a cart every year at the Bob Hope Chrysler Classic in La Quinta, California, once quipped: "It's not hard to find Jerry Ford on a golf course—you just follow the wounded."

My bet is that the former commander in chief would have been welcomed with open arms at the Navy-Marine Golf Course in Hawaii, and would have found it quite funny that the bartender there—who was no friendlier to me than the jarheads I had played with—named a vodka-and-V8 drink after me, the Bloody Damn Wuss.

PART

III

The Short
Game

CHAPTER 12

Putting Stroke Du Jour

I've always been too easily influenced. As a result, I'm on my 14th putting stroke of the season, with almost as many discarded putters. None of it has helped. I see someone sink a putt longer than 4 inches, and voilà! All of a sudden I'm imitating his stroke. If it works for that guy, why not for me?

Even as a kid, I was far too gullible. One Christmas morning I was in the backyard of our family's home, testing out the neat new walkie-talkie that Santa had brought me. "Hello? Hello? Can anyone hear me?" Giddy that my 6-year-old self might actually be able to communicate with the world at large, I eagerly waited for someone—anyone—to reply.

"Hello," the answer came quickly. "Who's this?" "This is George," I said, overjoyed that the world spoke back. "I can hardly hear you," the voice said. "George? You're kind of breaking up." I spoke louder: "I just got this walkie-talkie for Christmas!" "Ah . . . well, Merry Christmas," the crackly voice said. "Do you want to know how to make your new walkie-talkie work better so I can hear you?" I was by now ecstatic that not only could I communicate with other humans in this new world, but that this budding relationship was about to pay immediate dividends. "Sure," I answered, dumb as the morning was bright. "Just put it in a pot of boiling water for 10 minutes," he said. "That will clear everything up."

Needless to say, my Christmas gift was soon ruined. But do you think I learned anything? Apparently not; I'm still as easily swayed as ever. It's as if every time someone sinks a putt, I hear that fuzzy voice asking, "Wanna know how to make it better?" And I always answer, "Sure."

So far this year I've seen and tried a claw grip and a left-hand-low cross-handed grip. I've tried extending my right index finger down the shaft, pushing with two knuckles, looking only at the ball, looking only at the target, and putting sidesaddle. I've putted with a TaylorMade Rosa, a Yes! Golf Abbie, a bright turquoise-colored GEL Emerald, and a belly-length Callaway. I've even tried my wife's Odyssey Two-Ball. Same results, no matter what. I can push a 2-footer right, and I can pull a 2-footer left. I can do everything but roll it in the hole.

> I can push a 2-footer right, and I can pull a 2-footer left. I can do everything but roll it in the hole.

I played with one golf club general manager who had a surefire system: complete nonchalance. He'd stand behind the ball for just a fraction of a second to get a broad concept of the speed and break, then lazily one-hand a putt in the general direction of the hole. "The less I try, the better I putt," he said. And you know, he was pretty good doing it that way. So I tried it: nonchalant 2-footer left, nonchalant 2-footer right. Onward.

This summer in Colorado I watched my buddy Chris. He hunches over the ball like he is about to lay an egg, slides the knuckles of his index and middle fingers of his right hand down the grip, gets this knowing smirk on his big face and putts lights out. Looks dumb, but who cares? So I tried it: knuckled a 2-footer right, knuckled a 2-footer left. Onward.

I saw a guy on the practice green at my local muni one morning consistently dropping putts from 30 feet. He'd cradle the putter grip in the nook between the thumb and index finger on his right hand, stand tall, eyes over the ball, and create a lovely pendulum stroke. Plunk after plunk, into the hole. So I tried it: lovely pendulum 2-footer left; lovely pendulum 2-footer right. Onward.

Late in the fall, I went to see Chuck Cook, one of the best golf instructors in the country, down in Austin, Texas, at Barton Creek. He hooked me up to machines, shot some video, and immediately diagnosed the problem. "I want you to make a little forward press just before you take the putter back," he said. "That will stop the ball from skidding off the clubface. You'll get a truer roll and a straighter line." So I tried it: 2-footer in the hole. Bingo! Then another. Bingo! The man is a genius!

But that was 4 weeks ago, and besides, what always happens when you're in front of the doctor? Right: the symptoms go away. Nowadays, with a much truer roll and a much straighter line: 2-footer right; 2-footer left. Argh! Maybe the old sporting adage holds true: When all else fails, revert to the basics. So I'm thinking about boiling my new putter for 10 minutes—I've heard that clears things right up.

Practice Schmactice

A couple of weeks ago, I was scheduled to meet a friend for 18 holes. I showed up 10 minutes before our tee time, quickly paid in the shop, and hustled to the starter window. "Oh, your friend is on the driving range chipping," the starter said. "He's been there for an hour." "An hour?" I remarked, meaning something along the lines of: "What's wrong with him? Did he have a fight with his wife this morning?" The starter looked me up and down and said nothing. But I knew the look. He was thinking: "This guy is about to shoot a million. He could use some time on the range himself."

You see, there are two basic kinds of golfers: good and bad. Good golfers are typically the ones who practice, who enjoy going to the range a few times a week to groove their swing or work on their putting. They hit tens of thousands of practice balls a year. When you see them play, you admire their technique—even though you question their sanity.

Bad golfers, on the other hand . . . well, let's just get to the 1st tee. I count myself among the latter group. Practice schmactice. Show me a fairway, and I can miss it.

Good golfers were probably Boy Scouts growing up. They were those obnoxious kids in junior high who actually got good grades, did their homework, and ate their brussels sprouts. Heck, they probably even cleaned their rooms.

Bad golfers did none of these things. We questioned authority, were bored to tears in school, and thought football players and cheerleaders were bozos. We count as one of life's proudest moments the fact that we enrolled as Jimi Hendrix in our high school math class and answered "Present!" each day when the teacher called roll. We played frantic guitar music and sang—loudly—even though we couldn't hold a tune if it were clamped in a roach clip. (OK, maybe that last part was just me.)

Good golfers? They've read every instruction book ever written. They go to golf camps and schools, take weekly lessons, and do those ridiculous

> Good golfers were probably Boy Scouts growing up. They were those obnoxious kids in junior high who actually got good grades, did their homework, and ate their brussels sprouts.

practice swinging motions when standing there waiting for an elevator. The late Harvey Penick, esteemed instructor to many touring professionals, once remarked, "The good players are almost always the ones who ask me to watch them on the putting green. The high handicappers, who need it the most, would rather do anything than have a putting lesson."

Ben Hogan was a good golfer and thus believed in practice. "Every day you don't hit balls is one day longer it takes you to get better," he said. "The secret is in the dirt. Dig it out like I did." "The harder I practice, the luckier I get," Gary Player confirmed. And Sam Snead said, "I figure practice puts brains in your muscles." Still, I cannot seem to get excited about the secrets of Hogan's dirt or Snead's muscles. Sure, I'd like to play better golf, but c'mon. Hours and hours on the practice range is as exciting as painting a wall, cleaning the oven, or riding a stationary bike. Boooor-ing!

In his poem "America," Allen Ginsberg wrote, "When can I go into the supermarket and buy what I need with my good looks?" Indeed, why can't watching Tiger Woods on television make me a better golfer? Anyway, who said the object was to get better? I harbor no illusions about being a professional golfer. I'm still trying to play guitar and sing. My dogs cover their ears and howl every time I do, but I figure I've got to be good at something, someday. And it sure doesn't look like it'll be golf.

I've gotten to the point where if my game is above average, I'm proud. If most golfers in the United States don't break 100, as National Golf Foundation studies have consistently revealed, then my 82 last Sunday is pretty remarkable, no?

We're all good at something. It's just that the vast majority of us are not good at golf. Even Jack Nicklaus once quipped, "I just miss better than everyone else." Hogan, in his prime, said he typically hit but one really good shot per round. Holy 1 iron, Batman! If Hogan and Nicklaus are saying such things, that spells big trouble for me. Given that set of criteria, I'd be lucky to hit one really good shot per decade. So, practice? Uh, no thanks. My oven needs cleaning.

CHAPTER 14

Client Golf

People often say to me, "I'm going to take up golf—there's so much business done on the golf course." I hate to be the one to break it to them, but business is rarely done on a golf course. Funny business, maybe; serious discussions about widget orders or leveraged buyouts, no. It's against the rules. Not the *Rules of Golf*, published by the United States Golf Association or the Royal & Ancient, but, you know, the unwritten rules.

To be sure, there's a lot of "client golf" played. That's a game in which you lose $20 or $30 to your client, buy him or her a couple of beers over lunch, and hope that the bonding experience you just shared translates into new or continuing business. Someone must say the word "business" at least once during the round, just to satisfy tax regulations when trying to deduct the day as a business expense, but that's as far as it should go.

> Someone must say the word "business" at least once during the round, just to satisfy tax regulations when trying to deduct the day as a business expense, but that's as far as it should go.

Client golf is like your short game: it needs to be executed with precision in order to score. For example, whatever you do, never say, "So, Bobby, what can I do to get that widget order this year?"—particularly when Bobby is lining up his fourth putt for triple bogey.

Here are a few other keys to success when playing client golf:

1. If possible, never defeat your client. The caveat here is that if your client is a particularly miserable golfer, then losing to him or her might also be bad for business. In this circumstance, go ahead and win, but not by too much.

2. Never take money from your client on the golf course, even if you've made the mistake of winning. Pay for drinks and lunch. And if you are fortunate enough to have lost all the bets, pay quickly. Fast payment makes fast friends.

3. Take your guest to play someplace nice—but not too nice. You don't want to give the impression that you're wasting money. (And if you're the one driving to the course, don't arrive in a nicer car than the client's.)

4. Keep your demeanor civilized. Don't swear, throw clubs, or complain about drives 240 yards down the middle. Remember, "Eighteen holes of match or medal play will teach you more about your foe than 18 years of dealing with him [or her] across a desk."

5. Applaud your client's good shots, but don't lay it on too thick.

6. Win a hole or two so it doesn't look like you're purposely tanking the match.

7. Don't drink too much and start flirting with the cart girl or boy.

8. If you're keeping the score, always suggest par when asking what your client shot: "Three, wasn't it, Bobby?"

9. If you catch your client in a lie—"Yep, a three, Bill"—then watch your back in business dealings. (See rule 4.)

10. On the 18th green, always shake hands and say, "Great match. I look forward to playing again sometime," even if you have no intention of ever doing it again sometime and the only reason you did it in the first place was to curry favor and get that widget order.

The one time I found myself in an actual business situation on a golf course, I almost regretted it. It came about when I was applying for a job with a national golf magazine. I was set to meet my prospective employers in Pebble Beach, where the company was holding its annual sales meeting. Pebble Beach! Yikes! Talk about having to perform under pressure.

Not wanting to let on that I was really a mediocre golfer—not that it wasn't apparent when they saw me swing—I was hoping to break 100 when we played to discuss the job. If I could break 100 at Pebble, I reasoned, I had a good shot at the position.

The weather was good, so no excuses there. I hacked, and I hewed, and I hit some decent shots, too. I was sitting on 92 when we got to the tee of the final hole, a par 5 that invited disaster if any hole ever did. Playing my normal pronounced fade (read "banana slice") over the Pacific rocks on the left, I breathed a sigh of relief when my tee ball landed safely on the far right side of the fairway.

Next, however, in trying to shape a hairpin right-to-left shot around a tree—a maneuver far beyond my capacity, then or now—I sliced the ball out of bounds and came close to breaking a plate glass window on one of those multimillion dollar luxury homes that are blessed with such a perfect location. My heart sank as I contemplated the consequences of my ineptitude, but luckily my prospective employer thought that was pretty funny. With the 2-stroke penalty, I managed to pull a double bogey out of my back pocket (well, somewhere near there, anyway) and ended the day with a 99—and a job.

That was my first, and I swear my last, experience of doing business on a golf course. From that day forward, the only business I've ever done on a golf course has been monkey business. I suggest the same for you.

CHAPTER 15

Golden Golf: Till Death Do Us Part

I can't tell you how many times I've been beaten silly at my local muni by a 90-year-old guy named Saul, who bunts his tee shot down the fairway, dribbles a couple shots onto the green, and wobbles in his one-putt for par, all while I'm figuring out all too clearly the meaning of the adage, "The woods are full of long hitters," and chalking up another double bogey.

You know him. There are guys like Saul at every municipal course and private club in the world. He has been playing the game forever, has a set of Wilson sticks from 1953, and is still playing the same Top-Flite ball he pulled out 14 years ago. He can't lose the damn thing—he doesn't hit it far enough to lose sight of it, even though his eyesight isn't very good anymore. He can't damage it—he doesn't hit it hard enough. And he can't retire it. Why would he? A new one might change his luck.

Not that Saul needs any luck. He plays what I call "golden golf," and he'll play it until the day he dies. He plays nine holes every day, knows the golf course and every roll on it, knows everyone who plays or works there, and

> He has been playing the game forever, has a set of Wilson sticks from 1953, and is still playing the same Top-Flite ball he pulled out 14 years ago.

even gets a free round once in a while. It's only fair, I suppose. For goodness' sake, do the math. Saul is 90, so if he retired at age 65, that's 25 years ago. If he plays 360 days per year (taking into account a few holidays and sick days), that's 9,000 rounds. If he pays an average of $11 per round—the going weekday rate at our muni—that's $99,000 he's paid in green fees over the last quarter century. Holy bejeezus, give the guy a comp once in a while! No wonder he doesn't have new clubs and balls.

Not everyone wants to get paired up with Saul. I can understand. Playing a round with him can be frustrating, particularly when you've been beaten silly who knows how many times by his stupid little bunting game and his glacial shuffle down the fairway. I've contemplated this plenty of times, usually from two fairways over while looking for my ball behind the trees even as Saul stands bent over his stinking 150-yard drive in the middle of the fairway we're actually playing.

When I'm finally back within earshot, I usually ask, "Hey, Saul! Don't you get bored with always being in the middle of the fairway?" Normally, he doesn't respond, and I'm never sure if he's ignoring my feeble attempt at humor or if he's hard of hearing. It calls to mind my uncle D.D. Fuller—the "D.D." stood for Dufay Durias, a cruel joke my grandparents played on him—who would always tell us that he'd turn his hearing aid off when he came home so he wouldn't have to listen to his wife of 65 years go on and on about whatever it was he didn't want to hear about.

Is that what Saul was doing on the golf course? Tired of hearing *every* stupid golf joke and inane comment after playing daily for 25 years, did he just turn his hearing aid off? You couldn't blame a guy for that. Golf in blissful silence can be a wonderful thing—particularly for a short hitter in a group where every smartass in the deep woods has something to say to the guy in the fairway.

One day it occurred to me that I didn't even know Saul's last name or much of anything else about him. So the next time we played I asked him about his life, his work, and the like. Turns out Saul moved to California from Brooklyn in 1953, worked for years in the aerospace industry, retired in 1982, and got bored.

So he took up golf, a game he had always enjoyed but never played much. Soon enough, he was playing nine holes a day, and though over the years he lost more and more yardage on his shots, it was now about all he really looked forward to in life.

Saul is among many who feel the same way. Life for them is golf, golf, and more golf, with a few Grand Slam breakfasts and early-bird dinners at Denny's in between. Mostly, these are safe, predictable rounds where not much happens. Golf keeps our older citizens off the streets and out of gangs. But once in a while, we hear stories about the cruelty that age can bring to the game.

Consider the story of another 90-year-old, a certain Howard Tanner. Mr. Tanner scored his first-ever hole-in-one recently. Seventy-eight years after he teed up his first ball, Tanner finally dropped one in the hole on the 123-yard 9th hole of a course in Coconut Creek, Florida. Ironically, not one of the foursome he was with could see the ball drop. "I have very poor eyesight," said Tanner. "I seldom see where the ball goes."

Of course, age also has its privileges. One of the favorite stories at our course concerns a day when Saul was paired with a young man who was reluctant to go out with an older player, fearing it would slow him down. When they reached the 9th fairway, the young man found himself with a tough shot: There was a large pine tree right in front of his ball—directly between where his ball lay and the green. After several minutes of debating how to hit the shot, Saul said to him, "You know, when I was your age I'd hit the ball right over that tree."

With that challenge placed before him, the youngster swung hard and hit the ball right smack into the top of the tree trunk, whereupon it thudded back on the ground not a foot from where it had started. Saul offered one more sage remark: "Of course, when I was your age that pine tree was only 3 feet tall."

Recently, Saul has been missing from his daily round. I asked after him at the starter window, but they didn't know where he'd been either. We fear the worst. But then again—as with any marriage—with golf we have vowed, "Till death do us part." If it be so, may Saul be bunting with the angels.

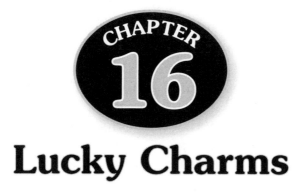

Lucky Charms

In golf, a good short game requires lots of practice and lots of luck. Since most of us eschew practice as if it were a rotting trout, it's the second part of the formula that we rely on most heavily. I think this true in all sports. Pistol Pete Marovich, the late, great basketball player, was known to wear the same pair of socks night in and night out if his team was winning. One can only imagine what Pistol Pete's locker smelled like.

Baseball players are known to be particularly superstitious. You see pitchers making a point of stepping over the foul lines—never on them—on their way to the mound, and batters flipping, twirling, and wagging their bats in the exact same manner before every pitch, all in mortal fear that if they varied their routine in the slightest their game would immediately slip into the seventh circle of hell.

Some baseball superstitions are more obsessive than others. Former Major League Baseball pitcher Greg Swindell, for example, was known to bite the tip off one of his fingernails before each start and hold it in his mouth the entire game for good luck. Wade Boggs, who during his career starred for both the New York Yankees and the Boston Red Sox, ate chicken before every game and took exactly 150 ground balls in practice. Slugger Larry Walker is known to be fanatical about the number 3: setting his alarm for 33 minutes past a given hour, taking practice swings in multiples of three, and wearing number 33 on his jersey. He was even married on the third day of November at 3:33 p.m., and he has 3 kids!

Golfers may be a little less obvious about their superstitions and lucky charms, but admit it—you have a few, don't you? Personally, I carry a polished, rose-colored stone from Glen Arbor, Michigan, in my pocket when I play. When I need a little extra juju on a shot, I reach into my pocket and feel the smooth, cool surface of the stone. This has a calming effect and also reminds me that even if I miss the shot the sun will still come up tomorrow.

I also practice what some might call hypnotherapy. I don't really care what you call it though; all I know is that it works. My preshot routine involves lightly pressing the thumb and forefinger of my right hand on the grip of whichever club I'm using and simultaneously letting a glacier blue color layer wash over my thoughts. I'm thus able to block out any distractions. People talking behind me, car horns blaring in the street, sirens screaming—none of it pierces my protected bubble of bliss.

Some golfers get a whole lot goofier than that. My friend Guy carries an acorn in his sock and is convinced it protects him from the wrath of the golf gods. Every now and then squirrels show a little too much interest, but Guy considers that a lucky sign. When walking to a tee box, Guy will never approach from the front or the back . . . always the side.

My friend Steve, on the other hand, is more a believer in good vibrations. His tool of choice: a Q-Link pendant that is worn around the neck. Advertised as "an advanced personal energy system*" that acts similar to a tuning fork and interacts with your biofield, Steve said his Q-Link was his "rabbit's foot" until one day he lost it. "Did your game go down the tubes?" I asked him. "Well, not really," he admitted, hesitantly, perhaps running an internal diagnostic on his biofield. He did mention he had just ordered a Trion:Z bracelet which he was convinced was going to help him accumulate more "minus ions." He wanted to see if that would help his putting.

I know a number of players who, if they are having a good round, will refuse to *clean* their golf ball for fear that their luck will change. And speaking of change, Jack Nicklaus is said to have

* Source: QeShop, www.qeshop.com

his lucky charms in the form of three coins he carries to appease the golf gods. Works pretty well for him!

Many professional golfers use coins minted in the 1960s to mark their balls on the green. The thinking? The coin will help them shoot a round in the 60s. Some golfers feel that even underwear is important. Jesper Parnevik, the edgy Swedish golfer, whose diet at one point in his career consisted solely of lava ash, revealed in a press conference a couple years ago that his wife bought him five new pairs of underwear just prior to a tournament . . . and he won. "Maybe that will be my new thing," he said. My motto is whatever works, but it does make you wonder: Boxers or briefs?

> I know a number of players who, if they are having a good round, will refuse to *clean* their golf ball for fear that their luck will change.

PART IV

The Mental Game

CHAPTER 17

The Parboiled Language of Golf

"Solid contact," said my friend Brown as we watched my drive sail from the 1st tee into the driving range on the right. Mulligan. "That'll play," he said about my reload as it was coming to a stop in the rough near the cart path, a hundred measly yards away. We hopped into the cart and drove to my ball. It didn't take nearly long enough. "Cart golf," he said when we got up to it.

"Not much you could do with that," he observed after I chunked it another 40 yards. "Pretty deep grass." At least it was on the fairway. "That won't hurt you," he offered, as I clubbed my next shot somewhere into the trees near the right side of the green. We drove up to his smirky little drive 250 yards out in the middle of the fairway. "Shot," I said, as he put it within 15 feet the pin. That's what the PGA Tour pros say. I don't get a chance to say it that often.

We went to look for my Slazenger. "I've been there before," Brown consoled. My ball was on a pile of pine needles under the trees, 35 yards over a bunker from a tight putting surface. "Nice shot . . . from there," he encouraged. I had luckily shoved it onto the back of the green, two tiers and three breaks from the hole.

"I'll send you a postcard," I told him, as I walked away to putt. "I think I'm in another zip code." "Can you see it?" Brown called over. His voice was faint and he looked kind of small from where I was standing, so I yelled back, asking him to tend the flag.

"Tough break," he said, after his birdie and my three putts, which resulted in a score I had to count on both hands. "You were robbed." Robbed of my dignity, maybe, but I deserved every bit of the triple.

"I'll send you a postcard," I told him, as I walked away to putt. "I think I'm in another zip code."

It was a typical day on the golf course. Brown was being courteous not to simply break out laughing at my misery. After all, it is pretty funny to watch someone hit a golf ball so poorly. It's not fun for 18 holes, to be sure, but fairly amusing for 2 or 3. Fortunately, I usually settle down into a bogey–double bogey mode after an outbreak on the initial hole. It's not great, but at least it allows me to say things like "Looked good in the air" to others when their wheels come off.

Golf has its own language. More than that, it has specific nuances that define the situation: "That'll play" (with a lilt). "Hammer time!" (emphatic). "You're in the fairway" (consoling). "You're on the dance floor" (approving). "Great concept" (enthusiastic). "We've got it surrounded now" (sarcastic). There are hundreds of phrases we've learned in order to cover every circumstance of the game—and only one way to say them properly. Even if you can't play a good game, you'd better be able to talk one.

"Nice lie," is one of my favorite sarcastic comments, jokingly quipped as my companion's ball is submerged up to its last dimple in the four-foot vertical face of a sand trap. Or I'll whisper, "Deer hunter. One shot—to the heart," as my soon-to-be-former friend is lining up a 7 iron to retrieve par from 150 yards out. This comment is invariably followed by a shank, and I don't mean a deer shank.

On the rare occasions when you really do want to make someone angry, try whispering "Kill it" when that person is on the tee. This bit of gamesmanship normally produces either a shoe-leaving, corkscrewing whiff—certain to open a rift between even the closest of enemies—or a feeble 100-yarder resulting from a too-conscious attempt not to overswing. You then say, "That'll play."

But you need to be careful. I've made late evening phone calls to friends hoping they weren't offended by one of my comments on the golf course that day. And every once in a while, after I've pleaded with some stranger's shot to "Get down!" or "Get in the hole!" I've been not-so-pleasantly asked to stop talking to their golf ball. Geez, it's not like the damn thing listens!

I've called my own tee shot everything from the Veg-O-Matic ("it slices, it dices") to the Mother of All Swings (a complete and utter catastrophe). I've referred to my long-iron game as Dog Bone (I take a divot so deep a dog could bury a bone in it) or the China Syndrome (a divot so deep I see Chinese faces staring back up at me). My flop wedges are usually just that—flops. And my putting normally requires conciliatory comments like, "Good speed. Thought you had it. You were robbed."

The worst thing of all after you've hit the ball is silence. That's when you know you've hit so many bad shots that day that your mates have exhausted their vocabulary. Silence may he golden, as the saying goes, but not after you've hit a golf ball.

It's the achy-breaky, parboiled language of golf. We're all experts and we know the parlance better than we know any other language, including English. Even Tiger Woods, just like us mortals, has his cute expressions: "Today I really rolled the rock," he'll say, referring to his putting stroke. Or he'll say, "The dots were nasty today," meaning the cup placements.

From time to time, we all do a Patsy Cline (fall to pieces) on the back nine or hit Jesus balls (they walk on water and require lots of prayer), rainmakers, dropkicks, infield flies ("run it out" is the requisite comment), tee shots that stayed in the air so long they needed flight attendants, dying quails, duck hooks, power fades, chili dips, fried eggs, duffs, and muffs. We've probably hit just about everything there is to hit—except, of course, fairways and greens. And we just can't say enough about that.

CHAPTER 18

Weapons of Mass Instruction

If you ask me, golf lessons are downright confusing. Today's piece of information invariably contradicts yesterday's. The thought process behind the shot I'm supposed to hit under one guy's tutelage is the polar opposite of what the last guy told me, and ultimately the whole exercise renders me incapacitated until I can drink enough tequila or get kicked in the head by enough donkeys to forget everything I've been told.

Maybe if I had started lessons as a kid I'd be more amenable today. Remember the silky pure swing of a 3-year-old punk named Tiger Woods on the *Mike Douglas Show*? But, no, I didn't take my first lesson until I was in my mid-30s, and by then it was far too late. I had two primary shots in my arsenal at that point: I could shank the ball 90 degrees sideways; and I could produce a magnificent banana slice off the tee—both feats I'm still fond of accomplishing once in a while, just for old time's sake.

My playing buddy at the time thought perhaps a couple of lessons would help, so he gave me a set of five. "Shank you very much," I told him. At the very least, he reasoned, my taking lessons might speed up our rounds, seeing as how it took damn near an entire day to shoot 150, my average score at that memorable point in my golfing "career."

Unfortunately, what my good pal failed to calculate into his equation was the "paralysis by analysis" factor. In other words, after lesson number one, my mind was so full of tips, pointers, reminders, mental images, hypnotherapeutic triggers—and fear—that I could barely swing at all.

I'd tee up a ball, stand over it, put my driver behind it, and freeze like a bronze statue in a city park. Like a flummoxed computer, my mind went straight to an error message. Let's see: I'm supposed to lock my knees, pretend my butt is against a wall, visualize a plane of glass and swing under it, make sure my left shoulder brushes under my chin in the backswing, keep my left arm straight, keep my fanny on the wall, keep my head still, think about hitting the tee and not the ball, pose in my follow-through . . . yikes! What was that third thing again? A pane of glass? Or smoke some grass? Or a pain in the—well, you know.

> I'd tee up a ball, stand over it, put my driver behind it, and freeze like a bronze statue in a city park.

The truth is I never went back for lesson two. It's just not in my genetic makeup to learn things that way. I'm more of a trial-and-error guy. OK, maybe more of an error-and-trial guy, someone who did not have a natural talent for golf, but who had all the gusto and bravado of outnumbered Scotsmen charging down a hill, swords held high, to do battle with a superior English foe who would surely slay them.

And isn't that more of what golf really is? A battle with a foe we'll never live to defeat? The title of Dr. Bob Rotella's book of insights gives us a good reminder: *Golf Is Not a Game of Perfect.* And I've been the living example of just how far from perfect we can be. I've tried it all. The absolute worst thing I can do for my game is sit down with a golf instruction magazine and read the game improvement features. I call these well-meaning stories "weapons of mass instruction." The cumulative effect of all these tips, drills, and "key moves" is utter chaos in my brain.

My good friends at *Golf Magazine* recently sent me a book titled *The Best Instruction Book Ever!* I fell in love with the exclamation point on the end of the book title, and in fact it was only because of that punctuation mark that I dared to open the covers of this handsome volume. I read the first page. It screamed "Your best golf ever!" and showed me a pretty sequence of swing photos.

But from that point forward nothing made sense. Maybe there were too many exclamation points. I read that the club should "swing itself!" That I should play the ball "even with my left ear!" That I should "position the ball at my left armpit!" That I should give it a "right-hand slap!" That my knuckles should be "down for power!" That my knuckles should be "up for control!" The next time I ventured onto a golf course I shot 150! Shank you very much!

At one point I thought that perhaps I could improve my game by mastering the mental side—you know, that maybe I was more "brainiac" than "brawniac." I read Rotella, and I read about Zen golf, zone golf, and purposeful golf. It turns out there are as many books and articles about the mental side of the game as there are about the physical side. Deepak Chopra's *Golf For Enlightenment* told me, "At the deepest level you can make shots worthy of a champion, while at another level you are a frightened beginner." He concluded, "No matter what you choose, play to be free."

For myself, I chose to put all the mental-side books back on the shelf beside the instructional books and thus be free in my own way. "How's that working for you?" you might well ask. Well, I'm a pretty happy camper, I must say. Far from perfect, to be sure—and still capable of the sideways and the monumental at the drop of a Titleist—but overall I'm just a blissfully instruction-free kid having fun in the green playing fields of the world. Shank you for asking.

Gamesmanship

The great Spanish player Seve Ballesteros—three-time British Open champion and two-time Masters winner—is also known as one of the greatest practitioners of gamesmanship that golf has ever known. The term *gamesmanship* refers to one's use of tactics that, though unconventional, are not strictly illegal: doing anything you can—within the rules of the game—to get in your opponents' heads, distract them from their focus, and thereby give yourself an advantage.

A few techniques from the master's playbook: Ballesteros was known to game other players by jingling change in his pocket while his opponent was making a shot, standing in their line of sight and shuffling his feet while they were putting, coughing when they were about to strike the ball, and starting his walk down the fairway while they were in their downswing on the tee.

PGA Tour veteran and two-time Ryder Cup captain Paul Azinger called Ballesteros "the king of gamesmanship" and verbally sparred with him frequently, most memorably over allegations of cheating during one particularly acidic Ryder Cup. Though many of his contemporaries grudgingly considered Ballesteros' antics fair and clearly within the rules, they often described the obstreperous player as having departed from the spirit of the game—not cheating per se, but operating as close to the edge as one can get.

But allow me to take Seve's side. If you ask me, golf is too damn civil. Don't you ever wonder why it's the only sport where heckling and trash talk never occur? Wouldn't you like to see hundreds of fans behind the 18th green, jumping up and down, waving yellow flags, and yelling, "Your mother has fleas!" as Phil Mickelson tries to set up a winning putt?

By contrast, gamesmanship as Ballesteros practiced it was pretty subtle. Yelling "Kill it!" during someone's backswing would have been flagrant. Clearing his throat was relatively gentle, even meek, in my book; it's more akin to a football coach calling a timeout to "ice" an

> If you ask me, golf is too damn civil. Don't you ever wonder why it's the only sport where heckling and trash talk never occur?

opponent's kicker before a field goal. I think we should insert some kickboxing into golf. We could make it a biathlon—18 holes followed by 15 rounds. The feature match would be Tiger Woods versus Phil Mickelson, and my money would be on the muscular Woods over the pudgy southpaw.

Greg Norman is a fan of good-natured gamesmanship: "Since I'm a long hitter, I like to have some fun with my opponents," he says. "Sometimes on an extremely long hole, if I'm hitting second, I'll take out an iron and lean on it as my opponent gets ready to play his shot. Occasionally I can actually see him thinking, 'This hole is 450 yards and Norman's teeing off with a 1 iron? My God, he must be even longer than I thought.' If I can get those types of thoughts going through my opponent's mind, he might do anything. Then when my turn comes, I put the iron back and take out my driver."

Norman says he also tries the opposite tactic: "On a tight hole where I know everyone's debating about club selection, I'll quickly take out my driver and waggle it a bit for everyone to see. The other guys then may make the mistake of selecting too much club for the shot. After they hit, I'll put the driver, which I had no intention of hitting, back in the bag and select a more intelligent club."

Norman admits that he himself has been outgamed. He relays this story of being bested by another gaming master, Lee Trevino: "During the 1986 U.S. Open, Lee got me good. At the 10th hole one day, each of us had a tricky downhill birdie putt. Trevino hit first, and when his putt finished a foot or so past the hole, he said to his caddie (for my benefit), 'Herman, that is the fastest putt I've seen all year long.' It worked. I left my approach putt 5 feet short and then missed the next one. Lee parred the hole and I bogeyed."

I like to think about what would happen if trash talk were used in golf. What if Norman added some taunting to his repertoire? Imagine him getting in Trevino's face all the way down the fairway: "The Shark's gonna kick your rear end, Merry-Man! You can't score on me. How do my cleats feel on your back?" In this light, a little coin jingling and coughing seem pretty mild, eh?

In a *Golf Magazine* interview, Ballesteros himself discussed his ability to game his opponents: "I love it if it's done fairly and inside the rules. Walking fast, walking slow. 'I'm away. No, you're away.' Or 'I'm 162 away. No, it's 163.' You can try to upset me by making me putt very short putts. Paul Azinger would look at me like I had marked the ball wrong or wouldn't let me use a new ball to putt with if the old one had a cut. All that is a fantastic part of the game."

If Seve liked tasting his own medicine, maybe the gamesman in your foursome will too. Next time you're playing against someone you think is gaming you—or even the next time your round gets a little monotonous—try one of Ballesteros' tried-and-true gamesmanship techniques. Or make up some of your own.

One of my personal favorites, which I employ when I'm playing someone I really want to beat, is the Maximum Disappointment Maneuver. Here's how it works. Let's say your foe has just struck a decent drive, but you see that it has edged off the fairway and into a bunker. Say just loud enough to be heard, "Position A." "Didn't it roll into the bunker?" your unsuspecting opponent might ask. "No, it's just fine," you'll tell him. "Position A." Then, as you stroll up the fairway, you compliment his swing. You say you've never seen him so smooth. When he arrives at his ball and sees it snuggled against a high lip: Maximum Disappointment. And voilà, you're in his head.

Another tool I use when my opponent is on a roll is playing extra s-l-o-w-l-y. This move often triggers impatience, and the next swing is likely to be choppy, at which point frustration sets in.

Clearly, then, there are many techniques to master in the dark art of psychological warfare. Ballesteros may be the acknowledged master, but you can do it too. After all, gamesmanship is not brain surgery. Or is it?

CHAPTER 20

E9

Some days are particularly lousy. Nothing goes right. The dog makes a big stinking mess on the carpet, you get a jury summons in the mail, every business contact you have laughs at your fantastic idea, and your computer goes on the fritz—again. Argh! You contemplate plucking your eyebrows out with a pair of pliers, combing your hair with a whipsaw, or at the very least getting into another line of work. Suddenly the phone rings.

"What!" you yell into the receiver, expecting an IRS auditor. "E9," the voice on the other end says calmly. Your blood pressure immediately drops 20 points. "Hallelujah," you reply. "An appointment with Dr. Green." "See you there," says the voice.

Thus an E9, or "emergency nine" (holes of golf), has been enacted, and not a minute too soon. You drop what you're doing (gladly), stuff your frustrations (along with your pliers and whipsaw) into the hall closet, and run to the car. Twenty minutes later, you're happy as a hound on a Thanksgiving dinner table, as you get ready to swing away on the 1st tee with nary a care in the world except hitting the fairway.

There are four guys in my group who can make the call to enact an E9: Jimbo, whose golf swing looks like he's doing the funky chicken, which by itself makes me smile; Gary, who, being a type A ad guy, probably calls the majority of our E9s; Tom, a bum, really, who is ready to go play anytime, anywhere; and me. I have a hard time admitting defeat even on particularly lousy days, so I probably call the fewest E9s. But when someone else calls one, I'm out the door in a heartbeat. See you later, honey. I'll be back in time for chow. Don't forget to let the dogs out.

There's an unwritten rule—under penalty of buying beers for all after the round—that during an E9 round no one shall discuss or inquire about the circumstances that prompted the call. There's no talk of dimwitted clients, unwanted jury summonses sent by Big Brother Who Is Always Watching, or pooch-soiled carpets that need shampooing sooner rather than later. In fact, sometimes there's no talk at all—just four guys puffing away on their stogies and walking into the sunset with golf bags slung across their backs, blissful on the afternoon golf course.

At other times, talk is brisk, but always frivolous. Not Britney Spears frivolous, but golf frivolous. "Ever wonder about those guys who dive into lakes on golf courses to retrieve golf balls?" Gary asked one day. A few stogie puffs later: "In South Carolina there are alligators in those lakes," said Jimbo. "How crazy do you have to be to jump in those looking for golf balls?"

The fact is I don't know much about Britney Spears, but, having lived in South Carolina for several years, I do happen to know a little about golf ball retrieval from alligator-infested lakes. "Some guy actually wrote a book about it," I said. "It's called *The Lost Golf Ball Book*. The author claims that the average player loses 4.5 balls per 18-hole round, most of them in lakes. It's a $200 million dollar industry retrieving them from lakes. The guys who do it call it white gold." "Sure," Jimbo said. "But what about the alligators?" "I'm told they don't bother you," I reassured him, "unless you look like a poodle. Then you're dinner."

Incidentally, for anyone interested in a career change, there's a franchise available through a company called ReTeeGolf, whose motto is Bad Golfers Are Good Business. The company's Web

> There's an unwritten rule—under penalty of buying beers for all after the round—that during an E9 round no one shall discuss or inquire about the circumstances that prompted the call.

site asks, "Do you currently dive in the ponds for golf balls battling against gators, turtles, fish, sludge, and grime to pick up golf balls by hand and wonder if there is a better way of doing this?"* If you are so inclined, and you have $3,500 to spend, the company will sell you a golf ball retrieval machine that will set you up for years and years of fun. Unless, of course, you look like a poodle.

Meanwhile, back at our E9, the four of us are by now yukking it up, telling stories—or maybe spreading urban myths—about poodles that wandered onto golf courses and were chomped by alligators, golf balls that were picked up by eagles and dropped near flagsticks, golfers who were run up trees by angry moose, and beautiful drives that disappeared down rattlesnake holes. It's a wild, wild world out there on a golf course. But some days that's exactly what we need.

* Source: ReTeeGolf, http://home.nc.rr.com/reteegolf/franchise_info.html

The Tyranny of Par

My fellow Americans, revolt! No, this is not a political tirade. It's a call to golfers. Par is a tyrant, and we've been trapped under its cruel and inhuman rule for too long!

I for one am of the opinion that we as Americans take all of our sports far too seriously. Too often, I've found myself moping around the house because my favorite basketball team, the Los Angeles Lakers, blew a 15-point fourth quarter lead and lost the game. And how many times, from fans in how many cities, have I heard the rabid chant "Beat LA! Beat LA!" I know, I know, we're a bunch of vapid, egotistical, self-absorbed bliss ninnies out here in California. But that sort of behavior is taking sports a little too seriously. It's just a game!

Golfers, I herewith issue a call for us to rise above the din! We can overcome. Let's stand together and realize we face a common foe, and that foe is par. Let's set an example. The other day, I was on the course with a friend named Kevin. Things started fine: 4, 4, and 5 meant level par for the first three holes. But on the fourth, a quick snap hook into the trees left Kevin in an impossible situation under some bushes.

> Let's stand together and realize we face a common foe, and that foe is par.

After declaring an unplayable lie, taking a drop, and chipping to the fairway, he was so rattled that he fatted his next shot. It sunk deep in the lip of a greenside bunker, with only a few dimples showing. Kevin hacked hard, and managed to dislodge the ball from its sandy grave. It valiantly tried to climb over the edge of the trap, then rolled back in. Trying to contain his utter contempt for the fates and everything about the insipid game of golf, Kevin got out on the next shot—and proceeded to three-putt.

The result of all this? A stinking 9 on an easy par 4, and what was, only a few fleeting minutes ago, a chance at perfection turned quickly into a typical day on the golf course. Several frustrated, less-than-perfect holes later, Kevin started playing better again. "You're back," I offered. "That's the guy we know." "I'm playing better now that I've stopped keeping score," Kevin said. Ah! The magic words! He had regained his composure—indeed, his sanity—as soon as the tyrant par had been banished from the kingdom of golf.

By contrast, golf in the homeland of Scotland is a wholly different animal. People play for the joy of being outside. Their goal is not perfection via making par. The favorite game across the pond is match play, and keeping score is simply a way of knowing who has won any given hole. They really don't care if they score a 9, as long as you score a 10.

In fact, on some days, in certain weather conditions, 9 might be a darn good score on a par 4 hole. Understanding that par is but a number—not a holy commandment—seems a far healthier approach to the sport. In the United States, we seem to think of par as the only acceptable score to shoot on a hole, regardless of weather, skill level, or emotional condition. We even go so far as to equate par with self-worth. If we are less than perfect— parfect—then we are less than worthy. We've paid our $150, and if we can't do it right, we might as well do away with our worthless selves. So I say, give yourself a break, fellow Americans; revolt against par. Think of par as a friendly suggestion made by the course architect.

In St. Andrews, Scotland, you'll find that the Old Course is closed on Sundays. Golf is but a game—not a religion—and it is not uncommon to see families using the hallowed fairways as picnic grounds with kids and dogs running freely about. Can you imagine that happening at your home course? Or at Augusta National?

In the homeland, golf is a game of the people, played by virtually everyone. Golfers typically walk the courses, using a pull cart or carrying their own bags. They don't need to play 18 to be satisfied; a 4-hole loop after work is just fine. A little exercise, followed by a pint or a wee dram o' Scotch at the local pub—isn't that an attitude we should emulate?

A round in Scotland is generally inexpensive, and there are few members-only courses. I have many Scottish colleagues who charge that in this regard we Americans have missed the point. Sure, we're building some excellent courses. Our designers, such as Tom Fazio, Rees Jones, Pete Dye, and Jack Nicklaus, are among the finest in the world. But the concept of expensive and private golf, ruled by the tyranny of par, goes against the grain of my old-world friends.

Golf, they say, was meant to be a commoners' game, simply a way to get a little hike or pass the time of day while herding sheep. So, America, do your best, but cool your jets. Unless your name begins with Tiger and ends with Woods, golf is not your livelihood; it's your downtime. So get down.

Remembering
Why We Play

The game of golf can be particularly frustrating or singularly exquisite. And the fact is, you have your choice. Frustration sets in when you have a bad day, right? You hit great shots but never get a friendly bounce. The ball lips out of the cup all afternoon, burns the edges, and walks the cellophane bridge. Or maybe you simply can't get those long irons anywhere near the target. Finally, around hole 7, you're ready to yank your hair out and throw your clubs in the nearest hazard. You wish your partner would shut up. And you probably wonder why you bothered to get out of bed for this masochism in the first place.

Does that describe you? If so, you've forgotten why you play the game. If you're really bad, take a lesson. But please don't take your 50-handicap rear end onto the golf course and expect to enjoy a round (or expect those playing with you or behind you to be happy). However, if you're like the majority of golfers, hovering between a 10 and 25 handicap, get

> Love your great shots and accept your bad shots. Try to improve, sure, but remember who you are.

real! You ain't no Jack Nicklaus, babe. Love your great shots and accept your bad shots. Try to improve, sure, but remember who you are.

A golf guru who gives many clinics to professionals and businessmen once told me, "Most people who come to my schools are completely in control in every facet of their lives. They are high-powered business executives who are used to making difficult decisions and being in charge. And yet when they get on the golf course they are suddenly confronted with a situation they cannot ever completely master: a small round ball that they are unable to control with the implements provided. They get frustrated by that, so the first thing I do is work on their heads."

At the other end of the frustration rainbow is happiness. That's where you'll find the pot of gold. One of the most enjoyable golf experiences in which I have ever participated—and one where our proverbial pot of gold was overflowing—was the World Writers Cup held in Palm Beach a couple of years ago. Ten golf writers from the United States were matched against ten from Europe in a three-day Ryder Cup format. Accommodations were provided by the historic and elegant Breakers hotel, and the teams dueled over the Champion Course at PGA National, Emerald Dunes, Breakers West, and the Breakers Ocean Course.

Sound like fun? It was. Although I did not play well that week (I tanked in my singles match 6 and 5 against Colm Smith, a perfectly delightful fellow who is a columnist for the Irish Independent newspaper group), I thoroughly enjoyed the company of my peers from this country and abroad. We all found new friends for life. To me, that's what golf at our level is all about.

Another group of folks finding the fun in golf are the Trashmasters. Their tournament, called the Trashmasters Invitational and held in Aspen every summer since 1993, is based on a simple concept: Play golf and have a blast. Remember when you used to do that? Trashmasters founders Lollie and Boone Schweitzer describe their event like this: "In an age when sports are taken very seriously and have become big business, there is still a group of guys and gals who love the game and truly play just for the fun of it. In fact, the crazier it is, the more fun we have."

The Trashmasters Invitational is won by the golfer who scores the most trash points during the course of his or her round. Now, I'm sure most all golfers are familiar with trash, but the Trashmasters have elevated it to a new level. Each team is "sworn in" on the 1st tee by Boone. With right hand raised, they swear to play "the trash, the whole trash, and nothing but the trash, so help me golf." Their points are then calculated in this manner:

- Sandie: Any par or better after hitting a shot out of the sand (1 point per sand trap recovered from)
- Drinkie: Any par or better after hitting into a water hazard (3 points)
- Barkie: Any par or better after the ball strikes a tree or any part thereof (1 point per tree hit)
- Watson: Any shot for par or better that is holed from off the green (3 points)
- Seve: Any par or better after striking a shot from the deep rough, aka "the Conga," which must be at least 6 inches deep (1 point)
- Skippie: Any par or better on a hole where the ball skips across a water hazard (1 point)
- Rockie: Any par or better after the ball strikes a rock of at least baseball size (1 point)
- Jerry: Any par or better after the hall hits an obstruction, including humans, bridges, outhouses, fences, sprinkler control boxes, signs, hotels, windows, condos, patio furniture, water coolers, rakes, course rangers, dogs, bears, automobiles, and any other obstructions (golf carts excluded) you can get your foursome to agree to (1 point per obstruction)

The tournament also awards points for greenies, birdies, net and gross eagles, and net and gross albatrosses. Bonus trash is given for multiple trash holes.

I applaud the Trashmasters! I like their intent. In addition to making the game loads of fun, they raise funds for educational scholarships and other charitable causes. Maybe their exact approach to golf isn't for everyone, but Michael Douglas has played, as has former vice president Dan Quayle, who said, "I'm not sure I'm really going to get—nor do I want to get—too accustomed to hitting in the sand, trees, or water. But we will do it for one day and have a lot of laughs."

As I see it, we really do have a choice. We can keep pulling the hair out of our heads over what may in reality be our best game, or, like Dan Quayle, we can have a lot of laughs and simply enjoy the game of golf—win, lose, or trash.

Open Letter to the PGA Tour Commissioner

PGA Tour Commissioner
100 PGA Tour Boulevard
Ponte Vedra Beach, FL 32082

Dear Commissioner:

I quit! My back hurts, I've got blisters on my feet, and I just shot my third straight 100-plus round. Golf is a stupid game. What am I, a complete boob? A moron? I hereby vow never to subject myself to another round of this insipid abuse. See you on the beach, old pal.

I'm addressing this letter to you because you're the guy in charge of the Tour, and I've been trying to emulate your players for so long it feels like forever. It looks so easy when Tiger and Phil play the game. But it's just not working for me anymore. My bowling ball has been retrieved from the closet and shined. I pumped up the old basketball yesterday, and my tennis racket now leans in the corner where my golf clubs were. (By the way, do you know anyone who could use a set of TaylorMade irons? I'll pass 'em along cheap.) I really can't believe that anyone takes golf seriously. I've come to agree with Mark Twain's analysis: "Golf is a good walk spoiled."

I'd also have to agree with the noted golf writer Jack Berry, who said, "You can improve your game 100 percent by

> I've come to agree with Mark Twain's analysis: "Golf is a good walk spoiled."

quitting." I'm taking that piece of advice, and I hereby reclaim my right to wander aimlessly through the fields and meadows of life without frustrating the bejeezus out of myself with inanities and banalities: "Is my left arm straight at takeaway?" "I wonder which way the ball will break as it rolls across the ridge?" and "Why do I hit it there every time I play this [bleeping] hole?"

It's late fall now, and I want the freedom to think more eloquent and poetic thoughts as I spend my time in nature. I want to delight in the fragrance of the turning leaves and the sway of butterflies in the autumnal air. I want to sit quietly and hear the birds busily preparing for winter in the trees, not blast them from their nests with hopelessly errant 9 irons.

I want to picnic under the majestic oaks with a fine bottle of Pinot Noir and some imported fromage, whispering sweet nothings into my honey's ear—not root like a misplaced hog after ears of muddy corn for my Titleist that is always blocked from the fairway by 10 trees or has come to rest under a thick bush. Do I look like a demented masochist to you? Or do I only act like one? "There is cruelty in golf—cold, hurting cruelty," said Henry Leach in 1914. "The difference between the effect of boxing and the effect of golf on the human system is that golf hurts more and the pain is more enduring, for it is psychological." I'm starting to catch his drift in a big way.

I've asked my friends if they can help me quit, sir. I believe an intervention is in order. They need to stop asking me if I have plans on Saturday and recognize that this is a sickness. I'm thinking of forming a local chapter of Golfers Anonymous. "Hello. My name is George, and I'm a golfer. I had an episode yesterday—I called for a tee time."

Maybe you need some help quitting, too? I know that as PGA Tour commissioner, and a traditionalist to boot, you'll have some trouble coming out of the closet about it, but just let me know. There must be legions of golfers across the land who need only a little encouragement in this matter so they can once and for all cease with the self-abuse and get on with the task of putting their lives back together. That's why I've decided to go public; perhaps I can serve as an example to others that this golfing habit can be beaten forever.

Mr. Commissioner, I hope you don't mind my candor here, but I've polished up my résumé and am forwarding it to *Outside* magazine. It states my employment objective thusly: "A writing job that involves communing with nature—no golf! I'm willing to relocate but cannot live within a 50-mile radius of a golf course." I hope you don't take this the wrong way,

but I can't go on like this. Thanks for
your understanding.

Sincerely,

George Fuller

P.S. Are we still on for 18 at Sawgrass
this weekend? I'll bring the straitjacket.

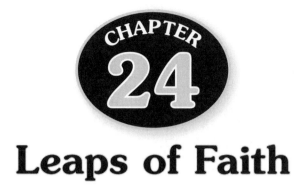

Leaps of Faith

Excuse me for a moment while I dance a jig like nobody's watching: I broke 80 yesterday for the first time in many moons! In fact, my game had been in the toilet, and I'd shot three consecutive rounds in the mid-90s. Things had gotten so bad that I wrote to the commissioner of the PGA Tour, announcing that I quit! Well, sports fans, *I'm back!* I've had enough of the "Hey, it's only a game" comments from my jaded friends to make me ill. Mates, take this as a thumbed nose. Look out long in the fairways and don't tread on my line to the cup. I've made another quantum leap.

These leaps are funny things. You never know when they're coming. You can get stuck on a handicap and not move it (the right direction is down, for all you sandbaggers) for months and sometimes years. Then, without warning, something clicks, something makes sense, and you feel a surge in your game and see a tight downward spiral in your index.

> Then, without warning, something clicks, something makes sense, and you feel a surge in your game and see a tight downward spiral in your index.

The first leap was the biggest, as I'm sure you remember: You shaved 20 to 30 strokes off your scores, seemingly overnight. In fact, for me at least, it did happen very quickly; then again, when I started the game, I had a long, long way to go. I suppose if I hadn't seen some improvement—however small—I might have blown off this crazy game altogether.

Luckily, in the early days of my golf career, I had a very patient and easily amused friend, Chris, with whom I'd hack around Waialae Country Club in Honolulu. My first rounds were in the 150 range; Chris shot in the 80s. Sandwiched between his bouts of laughing at my ineptitude—something I've since learned to do as well—we'd talk about golf. Chris would give me a few golf pointers and, since I was somewhat athletic to begin with, I was shooting in the 120s within several rounds.

Still, Chris was so confident in his abilities—he'd been golfing since he was a lad—and so bemused by my incompetence that he wagered $10,000 that I would not be able to beat him head-to-head in stroke play. The bet would last for a three-year period and would be contingent on our playing at least once a week during that time. I accepted the bet and set out to beat him.

My next leap took place after a couple of lessons and an assignment to write a guidebook on the golf courses of Hawaii. Two lessons, 80 courses, and 6 months later, I had my game hovering between 95 and 105. There it stayed for a year, and Chris was already counting my money.

Robert Bly, poet turned male bonding guru, has described how the imagery in his poetry requires leaps of faith to follow. Indeed, to jump from the wintry silence of a snowy field in Minnesota to the hollows of a man's heart does require a leap on the reader's part. Leaps in golf occur in much the same fashion. A word or two from a guru, such as my friend Rick Rhoads at San Francisco Golf Club, can often spur me to a new understanding of the game, and with understanding comes improvement.

Watching me club a few 7 irons into the woods off his practice range, Rick asked, "Do you take a divot before or after the ball?" I'd never really thought about it. "After," he answered. "The whole game is a matter of ball striking. If you hit the ground before the ball, your club will never be square at impact." Rick also moved me off the ball by a half step, allowing me to turn my hands over to work the ball right-to-left more effectively. "Look, turning your hands over extends the clubface by at least 6 inches. That's why you often hit the ball with the hosel when you try to hit a draw." Hmmm. Leap: 15.7 handicap to 13.3 handicap.

Dr. Mitchell Perry gives seminars to golfers. His message: "What you focus on expands. Focus on the positive and the positive expands. When many people hit a good shot, their first inclination is to ask, 'Where did that come from?' and when they hit a bad shot they say, 'I knew I was going to do that!' . . . Turn that around. When you hit a good shot, say, 'I knew I was going to do that!' and a bad shot only deserves, 'Where did that come from?'" Matt Leslie of the Myrtle Beach Golf Academy told me something else that made sense. "You're always told, 'Watch the ball,'" he said. "I add a few words to that and tell people, 'Watch the ball disappear from the clubface.'" I focused on it. Leap: 13.3 to 11.7

There are a million tips and insights about this game. The success of books such as *Harvey Penick's Little Red Book* derives from their ability to state the obvious in obvious terms rather than get complex with the blazingly simple. For the reader and player, the trick is being able to leap over that which you already know and allow your mind to assimilate new and better enlightenment. Penick's chapter "Take Dead Aim" is a perfect case in point: "Once you address the golf ball, hitting it has to be the most important thing in your life at that moment. Shut out all thoughts other than picking out a target and taking dead aim at it. A high handicapper will be surprised at how often the mind will make the muscles hit the ball to the target, even with a far-less-than-perfect swing."

The mind, the muscles, and the mythical perfect swing: Is there a single prescription that will meld these elements for every golfer? Certainly not. The game is no more singular or predictable than the universe in which it is played. Will it happen for every golfer? It will happen for most.

As for me, after breaking 80 yesterday, I'm publicly calling upon my old pal Chris to renew that $10,000 bet. Right now, I'm counting *his* cash.

Course Management

Golf or a Lime Exfoliation?

My wife Landry and I are different. On vacation, we both enjoy golf, but she'd much rather play nine holes and then beat a quick retreat into an orange-scented spa for a mango-papaya body polish or a cuatro manos (four hands) massage. Sometimes she'll skip golf altogether to get straight to the good stuff, like a kid who passes on the brussels sprouts to get to the dark chocolate. Me? I'm playing golf—all 18 holes and 90 (plus or minus) strokes of sheer frustration and occasional success. We're different, all right. She's smart; I'm a regular guy.

We found ourselves in exactly that situation on a recent trip to the Esperanza resort in Cabo San Lucas, Mexico. As I was sweating it out in the desert, playing Don Quixote with the cactus and my golf clubs, she was doing yoga under a palapa on the beach. She then moseyed to the resort's spa for her daily water ritual, followed by a grated coconut and lime exfoliation or hibiscus antioxidant flower bath, treatments that sound like they were invented long ago for the Queen of Sheba.

> As I was sweating it out in the desert, playing Don Quixote with the cactus and my golf clubs, she was doing yoga under a palapa on the beach.

When we'd meet back in our room around noon, she'd be calm and emit the pleasing aroma of fresh fruit. I didn't know whether to refrigerate her or nosh on her. I was angry and hot and smelled like a boar had just run me up the valley. The best idea was to take a shower and worry about it later.

While in Cabo, we did discover that we both liked Corona beer. Hers was in the form of a facial treatment; mine was in a longneck at the pool bar. This scenario plays out every time we travel, as I'm sure it does for many guys like me who have smart wives.

On another recent excursion, this time to Myrtle Beach, I was lured by the tremendous array of golf courses we all know about, and Landry was seduced by an equally tempting potpourri of spa treatments. That's not to say that smart women don't also enjoy golf; many do. But they will play one day and make a beeline to the spa the next—if not the same afternoon. So while I was hacking through the underbrush with my wedge at the Caledonia Golf & Fish Club, the Hibiscus Spa in the Marriott at Grande Dunes was pampering Landry with a seaweed body mask followed by a wild strawberry facial.

I'm welcome at the spa, too, I'm told, for some post-golf therapy to soothe my forearms, neck, lower back, and hips. But being a regular guy, I'm not always up for that. If they offered psychotherapy at the same time, I might go. "Doc, why is my wife always so happy and at peace with herself, while I'm frustrated and insane that I never break 80?" "Basically, sir, she's smart, and you're a regular guy. Now roll over; I'm going to crack your back." See how this works?

The next day, Landry indulged in a warm marine mud wrap at the spa, as I froze my tushy in the morning fog on the resort's golf course. She followed her wrap with a sea mineral exfoliation and massage, something I was getting the natural way out on hole 15.

We moseyed on down the coast to Hilton Head Island. In Harbour Town, I had quite a few choices of masochism: I picked Harbour Town Golf Links, just because it hosts the PGA Tour's

Verizon Heritage Tournament and I wanted something adequately humiliating. Landry, on the other hand, enrolled in a Diva for a Day package at the local day spa, which included a facial, a Vichy shower, and a Sedona clay wrap that gave her skin a "vitamin cocktail" by means of a rich body cream. I was ready for a cocktail, all right (or five) to help me regain my composure after those triple bogeys on 17 and 18.

I've concluded that spa directors are like chefs for the flesh. Just like their kitchen counterparts, they use local ingredients (mangoes, seaweed, and pumpkins), cook up elaborate schemes to tempt and please (wraps, polishes, cocoons, and massages), and offer it all on a smart-sounding menu. Spas, I've come to discover, are quite civilized places; golf courses, not so much.

On golf courses, you get sweaty, dirty, and irritated. Your playing partners will empty your wallet and laugh about it gleefully. Golf is like an artichoke facial with the thorns left on. Not only is it painful, but it leaves deep scars as well. Spas do the opposite. If I wanted to do the smart thing—a concept that generally escapes golfers altogether—I'd join Landry in the spa. My golf game might still stink, but I'd smell like a rose, or a pomegranate, or a papaya . . . .

March of the Haggis

Golf and food seem like such a natural combination: Play golf, get hungry, beat chest, eat. Somehow, the Scots—who invented the game as we know it—never got the concept. Most food you eat in the old country is—well, let's just say it's less than appetizing. The food for which the Scots are perhaps most famous, or infamous, is of course haggis. The words "Oh, God no" come to mind every time I think about my encounters with haggis, a "food" I'd be happy to never see again.

For those of you who haven't had the pleasure of savoring this Scottish dish, haggis is sheep's heart, liver, and lungs minced with onion, oatmeal, suet, spices, and salt; mixed with stock; and traditionally boiled in the sheep's stomach for about 3 hours. Excuse me; I need to go call Ralph on the white porcelain telephone. No wonder they also invented Scotch whisky—to wash down the haggis.

CBS broadcaster David Feherty, an Irishman by birth and a former professional golfer, described haggis in his novel *A Nasty Bit of Rough* as "pickled genitalia, minced eyelids, and shredded nostrils all wrapped up in a sheep's bladder and boiled for hours." Make that a triple Scotch whisky, please. I'd prefer to be blinded by flaming arrows than eat another forkful of haggis.

> I'd prefer to be blinded by flaming arrows than eat another forkful of haggis.

Still, there have been times when I was forced to cut and push some of the disgusting stuff around my dinner plate, and, under the watchful eyes of Scottish hosts, even insert a wee bit into my not-at-all-excited piehole. Golf in Scotland, good; haggis, bad. I was invited to the Westin Turnberry Resort on Scotland's Ayrshire coast a couple of years ago to celebrate that revered golf resort's 100-year anniversary. After several days of music, revelry, and amazing golf (despite the fact that I lost every match) came the final night's send-off bash. What was on the menu? You guessed it.

Haggis is traditionally served with great fanfare in Scotland—mostly, I suspect, to naive Americans and unfortunate losers of golf matches—and Turnberry's haggis ceremony was quite a spectacle. The march of the haggis from the kitchen to the dining room started with a bagpiper, audible from a distance, who marched down the stately hallway of the hotel and into the library dining room where we were seated. A gentleman with several bottles of fine single-malt whiskey followed the bagpiper, rotating the bottles over his head like he was peddling a bicycle with his uplifted hands. Behind him in single file marched the haggis bearer, proffering the vile bag of boiled entrails on a tray, and a bloke in a kilt, wielding a sharp knife and looking rather possessed.

The kilted guy demonically wielding the sharp knife over the haggis stood at the head of our bemused and slightly fearful table, and in his lilting, completely incomprehensible accent recited Scottish poet Robert Burns' poem, "Address to a Haggis":

> Trenching your gushing entrails bright,
> Like ony ditch;
> And then, O what a glorious sight,
> Warm-reekin', rich!

Now that's exactly how I like my food: warm, reeking, and rich. What the above poem translates to, roughly, is this:

I'm a crazy man speaking English
Even though you cannot understand me.
Eat this haggis or I'll slit your throat
with this knife and boil you for three hours.

And thus, I nibbled, fearfully and with deep regret, a very wee bite, as my gracious Scottish hosts looked on and smiled knowingly.

Still, though the Scots do not seem to understand, golf and food really are good companions. On this side of the pond, for example, golf and food traditions include the Tuesday night Champions Dinner during the Masters Tournament each spring in Augusta, Georgia. The previous year's winner hosts the event and selects the menu, and all previous winners are invited. First suggested by Ben Hogan in 1952, the menu often reflects the personality of the golfer who has the honor of hosting. Here's a sampling:

- In 1998, 22-year-old Tiger Woods treated his elders to cheeseburgers, French fries, and milk shakes.
- In 2004, Canadian Mike Weir selected elk, wild boar, Arctic char, and Canadian beer.
- In 1996, Texan Ben Crenshaw hosted a good ol' Texas-style barbecue.
- In 1986, German-born Bernhard Langer brought in wiener schnitzel and sauerkraut.

Mostly, the menus are selected in good fun and accepted by all as an opportunity to indulge in and enjoy the cultural differences of the world's best players. The former champs, however, are not required to eat what the defending champion selects; they can also order from Augusta National's regular dinner menu. Only once, I'm told, has there been a run on the regular menu. That's right: A Scotsman, Sandy Lyle, won. And he served haggis.

Shark Versus Bear

New golf courses typically open with a grand shindig or high-falutin hullabaloo. The developers, city fathers, various local dignitaries, and golf course architect are all on hand, engaging in various forms of mutual admiration and self-congratulation. Enthusiastic speeches, back slaps, and incomprehensible inside jokes are most often accompanied by a chafing dish heaped high with hard-scrambled eggs and another laden with deeply greasy bacon. Nearby, a few canisters of weak coffee tempt the desperate, and a straw basket or two of rather aged-looking pastries may lurk. Being a seasoned brouhaha attendee, I usually stop at Starbucks for a venti iced chai, nonfat, nine pumps. "Can I get something started for you?" You bet—I'm on my way to a golf course opening.

Usually, after the questionable cuisine and formalities, the golf course architect invites the gathered group to stroll the fairways with him. He struts to and fro like a proud peacock, a microphone clipped to his lapel, discussing every facet of his brilliant design. He waves his arms around in the air and points at distant land movement. He speaks of "shot values," "strategically placed bunkers" and "driveable par 4s," magnanimously addressing us as if we could actually break 100 or hit a drive out past 200 yards.

Some course openings include a full-blown exhibition match featuring current pros and legends. In fact, the legends format produced what may be the worst golf hole Jack Nicklaus ever played, and I was there to witness it.

Perhaps you recall *Shell's Wonderful World of Golf*, the charming televised series of golf matches that started back in

1962 (with Gene Littler battling Byron Nelson at Pine Valley Country Club in New Jersey) and ran through 1970, when it went on extended hiatus. In its early years, the Shell series produced some memorable matches, such as Nicklaus versus Sam Snead at Pebble Beach in 1963; Ben Hogan versus Snead at Houston Golf Club in 1965; and Don January versus Christy O'Connor at Royal County Down, Ireland, in 1968. When it was revived in 1994, the show became more of a promotional device for golf course openings. The courses paid dearly for the exposure, though perhaps not as dearly as those unfortunate souls who braved the scrambled eggs and bacon.

> The legends format produced what may be the worst golf hole Jack Nicklaus ever played, and I was there to witness it.

It was in the spirit of *Shell's Wonderful World of Golf* that we were on the little Hawaiian island of Lanai. Two of golf's greatest players, Greg "the Great White Shark" Norman and Jack "the Golden Bear" Nicklaus, came to Lanai to play an exhibition match to celebrate the opening of the Experience at Koele, a course Norman had co-designed on the island with Ted Robinson.

On hole 8 (which nowadays plays as hole 17), Nicklaus learned firsthand why the course is called "the Experience." As the signature hole on the course, number 8 features tee boxes cut at the top of a steep hillside, and the fairway drops to a distant swath of green grass 220 feet below. The hole is bordered along the right side by a sprawling lake they might as well have named Waterloo (since so many golfers meet their downfall there) and on the left by a hillside thick with underbrush. Said hazards demand of the player a straight and long tee ball, an exciting shot for any mortal golfer, and so it was on this day for Greg and Jack.

The Shark was first on the tee. After his characteristic waggle (at which a good many women in the gallery, eyes fixated on his behind, oohed and aahed), Greg proceeded to hook his tee shot into the hillside left. The Golden Bear did the same (though without the oohs and aahs).

Someone in the gallery yelled, "Mulligan!"

Everyone laughed and the golfers re-teed. The Shark then placed a drive in the middle of the fairway. But Jack—golf's immortal Golden Bear—proceeded to kiss six consecutive "aloha balls" into the lake on the right, claiming through clenched jaw that it was a "hit-till-you're-happy" hole, before finally steering his 14th shot into the fairway below. "Who designed this damn hole, anyway?" Nicklaus quipped as he and Norman left the tee box. We all laughed politely but could see that Jack's face was a bright shade of red. Someone in the gallery answered as they passed, "Well, after all, Mr. Nicklaus, it is the number one handicap hole!"

A few minutes later, as Nicklaus putted out for an 18, the gallery breathed a collective sigh of relief, as happy as he was that the hole was done. On the walk to the next tee, however, I overheard a young reporter, notebook and pencil at the ready, ask, "Mr. Nicklaus, was that an 18? What happened?" Nicklaus stared straight at him and deadpanned, "Son, weren't you watching? I missed the putt for 17," then turned and walked on.

I've had the occasion to interview Nicklaus several times since that day, but I've never brought up that rip in the space-time continuum. Can you blame me? To him, carding an 18 is probably a memory that ranks in his forgettable file right next to bad eggs and bacon—and that kind of memory, my friend, I wouldn't want to force on anyone.

Golf in the Middle
of Nowhere

People talk about golf spreading to the very ends of the earth, and a nine-hole layout on the island republic of Nauru—an 8-square-mile tidbit of land in the middle of the vast Pacific Ocean—proves the point. Unbearably hot and stiflingly humid during 10 months of the year, and desolate all 12, Nauru is a mere hiccup of land that surfaces above the ocean 36 miles south of the equator, midway between Guam and Brisbane, Australia.

Where? Exactly. If any place on earth deserves the official designation "End of the Road," or "Middle of Nowhere," Nauru is it. Located roughly 1,000 miles southeast of Guam and about 1,200 miles west of Papua New Guinea, and situated between (but not really near) the Marshall Islands, Kiribati, and the Solomon Islands, Nauru would certainly be in the running for possessing the most far-flung golf course in the world.

> If any place on earth deserves the official designation "End of the Road," or "Middle of Nowhere," Nauru is it.

The island's story is equally unlikely. Nauru first blipped on my radar screen in the late 1980s. A journalist, I was living in Honolulu and was "mad about islands," as author James Michener once described those of us afflicted with a passion for the tropics.

At that time, Nauru was building condominiums in Hawaii in an effort to forestall the collapse of its economy.

The big joke was that the Nauruan economy was based on the mining of phosphate, which really meant "crystallized bird poop," and we found it funny that an economy could be based on such an absurd thing. Apparently, seagoing frigate birds had used the faraway island as a stopping and dropping spot for many centuries. Over time, the buildup of bird guano had crystallized into phosphate, and the mining and sale of this phosphate had represented about 100 percent of the tiny republic's economy. Problem was, by 1989 the finite phosphate supply was dwindling, and in an effort to diversify its economy, Nauru made international investments. Thus the building of condominiums in Hawaii and office buildings in Australia (where most of the phosphate was used as fertilizer), as well as investment in theater productions in London.

When the opportunity arose for me to visit Nauru in the mid-1990s, thanks to a stopover leg on a flight that went to several small Pacific island destinations, my curiosity was piqued. My flight landed at 3 p.m. on a sweltering August afternoon and was scheduled to leave only a few hours later. A few people were milling about the funky airport; some were sitting in a sleepy bar watching New Zealand television. I inquired what there might be to see nearby. Well, one gentleman shrugged, not much: the phosphate loading dock, the Menen Hotel, Anibare Bay, a golf course.

Golf course? My ears perked up. This was strange. A golf course? Here?

The island had one road and, as far as I could tell, just one taxi to take whatever lost soul ended up here around the 12-mile circumference. Like Guam and Saipan, Nauru possesses one of those suffocating environments where your clothing becomes soaked with sweat in the time it takes to close your front door behind you. I hired the taxi, hoping (foolishly) that it was air-conditioned. The driver, watching me sweat in his rearview mirror, said the golf course was only a few minutes away, near the Nauru Phosphate Corporation (NPC) buildings, next to the power station. Our short route led through an area generously called the "capital city of Yaren," where Nauru's government offices are located.

The modest homes in this district are, like all the buildings on Nauru, constructed chiefly of cinder block to prevent them from blowing away in a tropical storm. Most homes had dirt yards filled with trash that was too expensive to ship away. There is no natural source of water on Nauru; it is brought in from Australia, as is just about everything else.

No water. Hmmm. And no grass in sight. My expectations of the golf course—not real high to begin with—diminished further. The road led inland a bit from the ocean, and (don't blink) there was the course. To my surprise, there was a little grass after all. I asked the taxi driver if he could return in an hour, but he decided to stay and wait. Guess there were no other potential passengers on the island that day.

I entered the cinder-block clubhouse, open on all sides to take advantage of any wayward breeze that might take pity on this island, and asked about the course. Joe, the fellow in charge, told me the course had nine holes: eight par 3s and one par 4. It was built by the NPC (controlled at the time by the British and Australians) after World War II as an amenity for NPC's staff and workers. There used to be a couple of Australian pros who would hang around, but they were long gone. Did I want to borrow some clubs and have a go?

The afternoon sun was weakening, and I had some time to kill. "Sure," I said, "How much?" "Oh, there is no fee," he said. "Enjoy it." Protruding from the trolley (pull cart) I was assigned, there was an odd implement that Joe described as a "scraper." I inquired. "Just clean up after yourself when you're done on the scrapes," he said. "Scrapes?" I asked. "You know . . . where you roll the ball . . ." He made a putting gesture with his hands. I soon found out what he meant. There was a bit of hardpan grass in the fairways, all right, but the putting surfaces were all bumpy white sand. You couldn't call them "greens," I suppose, since that color was nowhere to be found. So "scrapes" it was.

I played several holes, following out to where the course crosses the main highway and plays on the seaward side. I was surprised that there were no ocean views, given that the island is so small, but it's also pancake flat and there were houses in the way. Since I was more interested in looking around than actually playing the course, I walked the rest of the holes, then headed back to the clubhouse.

A few players had just finished, so I approached them. "And how did you gentlemen end up here?" I asked, not wanting to be rude but certainly curious who would be playing golf in this bleak place. "We're with NPC," one of them replied in a clear Australian accent. "Must seem strange to you, eh, mate?" I nodded. "It's not so bad," he said. "We're here for a year, make some good money, drink a few pints. And look—we even have a golf course! The only problem is when we have a good rain. Then the scrapes wash away. But it's all right; we just go down to the beach and get a new load of sand."

He told me a golf team from Nauru—composed chiefly of Australians who were on the island to manage the mining operations—occasionally participated in tournaments in Fiji or on Guam. But the big days at the Nauru Golf Club were Wednesdays and Saturdays. All the golfers from NPC play in the Saturday games, he said, whereas Wednesday's "chicken run" draws more locals.

"Chicken run?" I asked. "They play for chickens on Wednesdays," he said. "Used to be cooked chickens, but those winnings never made it home to mum. So now they play for frozen chickens. It works out much better that way." I told him I'd suggest that to my regular foursome back home and he laughed, knowing how odd it must seem to me. Soon enough I headed back to the airport, looking forward to catching my flight out.

After my visit, Nauru's story got weirder still. The international investments—particularly the London musical—flopped. The national airline, Air Nauru, was forced to ground flights for a time because it had fallen behind on the payments for its only plane. So, in desperation, the island passed laws that made it a haven for international money laundering and tax evaders, particularly the Russian mob. Nowadays, the phosphate is all but gone, and so too are Nauru's prosperous days. What happens next is anybody's guess. One thing, though, I'll guarantee: Nauru is not the next big golf destination. I was glad to see Nauru, and equally glad to leave.

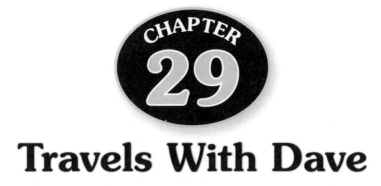

Travels With Dave

"We'll look back and laugh about this some day," said Dave. I had to admit, it was pretty funny already. My brother and I were speeding away from the Seattle airport, barely an hour into a 7-day golf journey through the Pacific Northwest. What we would look back on and laugh about some day was the hour we'd just spent at the airport rental car desk, trying to figure out just what the heck had happened to our reservation for a van.

Dave and I enjoy hitting the green highway with our sticks as often as we can. We've been making one extended golf journey per year for the past couple years, and with all our worldly cares safely swept under the rug back home, it's always a blast. The scene at the rental car desk at the airport proved one thing: With us, getting there is not only half the fun, but half the craziness, too. You see, Dave is completely useless when it comes to planning. Bless big bro's heart, but he's an attorney. In other words, he can't do a thing for himself.

Being the "golf guy" in the family, my charge was setting up the tee times and the accommodations, which, with careful months of planning, I managed to achieve without a hitch. Dave, on the other hand, was charged with just one simple task for the trip: arrange a rental vehicle large enough for us, our two pals, and everyone's golf clubs and luggage.

> With us, getting there is not only half the fun, but half the craziness, too.

Given that Dave is a helpless attorney, I should have known that even this relatively simple job was too much without the aid of an executive assistant. And indeed, when we arrived at the airport, there was no van reserved. Turned out that Dave had booked one in Portland, a mere 8 hours away. So, $800, 60 minutes, and a whole lot of raised eyebrows later, we drove away from the airport in an SUV so small we had to tie our golf bags and luggage on the roof. And we hadn't even picked up our two friends yet.

Over the course of the following week, we planned to play courses in Tacoma and Cle Elum—which is why we flew into Seattle—then drive south to Oregon, stay and play a few days in Bend, then head to Bandon Dunes over on the Oregon coast, where three of the finest links in the land are found. So far, so good: We hadn't even made it out of the airport and already we had a story to tell.

The centerpiece of our June excursion was the opening of a new Tom Fazio course at Pronghorn—one of the Bend area's most exclusive golf communities—and the debut of the property's spectacular new clubhouse. Pronghorn spared no expense. The wine and spirits were flowing like rivers, and the chefs were cooking up mountains of food. Joe Montana and Mia Hamm—both Pronghorn homeowners—flew in, and Kenny G gave a stirring Saturday evening concert at sunset.

The kicker for me, though, was the Las Vegas dance band that came on after Kenny G. Their cover songs from the 1970s and '80s were apparently right up my 58-year-old brother's power alley. Normally a bit, uh, stiff when it comes to letting his hair down and kicking up his heels, Dave was out on the dance floor— a few glasses of Oregon Pinot Noir (and maybe a lemon drop or two from the vodka bar) under his belt and a big Dominican stogie in his jaw—bobbing and bouncing with the dance floor crowd like he was 21 again.

My amusement turned to pure joy when, above the din, I could clearly hear Dave's not-so-on-key voice bellowing, "I love rock 'n' roll! So put another dime in the juke box, baby!" And when my

eyes caught sight of him, I saw my brother had all but comman-
deered the microphone from the band's lead singer, though in
Dave's defense all of us were feeling rather jubilant that night.

After golf the next day, we had car trouble as we were leaving
Bend and heading for Bandon. The steering started feeling very
rough, like it was about to go out, so we went to trade in the SUV
for a spacious van. As we were unloading our golf bags from the
roof of the SUV, the rental agent inspecting it asked, "Have you
checked the 4WD?" "4WD?" Dave and I looked at each other
dumbly. "Yeah," the agent said. "Looks like you have the 4WD
button pushed. That'll give you steering problems."

That's when the proverbial light bulb went off in my head,
and I remembered pushing every button on the dashboard the
previous day looking for the windshield wipers. Graciously, after
a simple push of his index finger solved our "steering problem,"
the rental car agent allowed us to drive off in the comfy new van
anyway, with our golf bags properly stowed inside the vehicle,
golfer style.

We finally arrived in Bandon late that night, then rose with
the roosters for a 36-hole day. That's a workout, particularly for
old guys like Dave and me. I was so tired after playing Bandon
Dunes that I dried my face with the closest thing I could find in
the clubhouse men's room. Too bad it was a toilet seat cover!
Like I said before, getting there is half the craziness. Being there
is the other half. And then there was the time . . .

30

Dreaming My Dreams

My old pal Brett called recently. We hadn't spoken in a while. "How are you?" he asked.

"Well, right now my head is at the Beach Bar at Mauna Kea drinking a mai tai after a round of golf," I told him. "But my body is stuck in front of my computer screen until June." It was only February, so things were looking pretty bleak as far as getting to the tropics anytime soon.

Years ago, Brett and I had had some serious laughs at the Beach Bar after playing golf, and I knew the thought of those magical moments would instantly transport him back to that seductive, crescent-shaped beach on the Big Island of Hawaii.

"Stop!" he cried. "You're driving me crazy." The thought was too much for him to take on a dreary winter day when neither of us had any hope of catching a flight.

We chatted a bit more and hung up, but I was useless for the balance of the day. I could just as easily have been distracted by images of Mount Juliet, Ireland; Pinehurst, North Carolina; Turnberry Isle Resort, Florida; or any number of delightful golf havens around the globe. The effect would have been the same: a complete inability to concentrate on the tasks at hand. And on the day Brett called, the tasks were many.

For me, dreaming the dream is fine—I'm capable of frittering away hours with nothing but palm fronds and putting surfaces dancing in my head—but actually making plans to go is even better. So, soon after Brett called, I shut my office door, pulled the calendar off the wall, and started plotting strategy.

x

x

Let's see . . . June is so far off. Maybe I could find some reason to go to the Arizona desert for a long weekend in February after all. Haven't been to the Phoenician in a while—and gosh, the Boulders is a must-visit while I'm there. And you know what? The Four Seasons at Troon North just did those renovations. Clearly, a long weekend wouldn't be enough time. Well, I could always cancel that meeting the following Monday and push the deadline on that story a few days. I was off and running, plotting like a teenager looking to score on prom night.

> I'm capable of frittering away hours with nothing but palm fronds and putting surfaces dancing in my head—but actually making plans to go is even better.

Hmmm . . . What's the weather like this time of year in New Mexico? The Inn of the Mountain Gods sounds like my kind of place. And getting back to Santa Fe for a stay at the Inn of the Anasazi and a few rounds of golf at the enchanting Las Campanas property—well, who could pass that up? My day was getting better already.

I have two main goals when I slip into this kind of planning. First, I want to visit places I haven't been to before, destinations with a reputation for great golf and first-rate accommodations. Second, I want to return to those tried-and-true favorites, such as Mauna Kea Resort, that never disappoint. The list goes on, and each year it expands. My eventual goal, of course, is to merge the two lists in the sense that I will have visited all the best golf resorts in the world and will then have a longer list of tried-and-true favorites from which to choose.

I know a fellow by the name of Glen who has been doing exactly this type of travel for several years. I first met Glen on the Hapuna Golf Course a couple of years ago when he was on his yearly Hawaii swing. Since then I have received regular postcards from Glen, letting me know where he is in the world.

He always ends with that ubiquitous phrase, "Wish you were here teeing it up with me." Me too, Glen!

As I write this, Glen is in Cabo San Lucas, Mexico, playing golf and watching whales jump. I know because a new postcard arrived just yesterday. I think this is Glen's way of sticking his tongue out at me and saying, "Nah nah-nah nah nah nah," like a 6-year-old might do when trying to drive another kid nuts. And it works; Glen's postcards always drive me batty.

But one day it'll be my turn, and while others are stuck in front of their computer screens, I'll be chasing pars, sunsets, whales, mai tais, and memories, just like Glen. And driving Brett crazy with postcards.

CHAPTER
31

Whipped by the Master—Again

Some courses just bust your booty, each and every time you play them. You may have scored in the low 70s the last five times you played elsewhere, but when you get to one of these special places—BLAMMO!—upper 90s, every damn time.

Pull into the parking lot, and everything goes straight downhill. You can't even extract your clubs from the trunk without smashing a finger or denting a shin. Once on the course, you can't hit a fairway, you can't hit a green, and you're three- and four-putting from 5 feet. Absolutely nothing goes right all day. You probably even burned yourself with a lit cigar last time you were there.

Meanwhile, your buddies are having a grand old time. They're laughing, scoring like squirrels on a nut farm, enjoying your struggle, and asking things like, "What's wrong with you buddy? You look like a skunk crawled in your cubbyhole and let loose. You should see the look on your face!" The bozo in the group will even try to show you what you look like by wrenching his own face into a painful twist. Thanks.

Every shot may make someone happy, as the saying goes, but on this course, none of those someones is you. There may be "courses for horses" as another saying goes, where you shine like a tree ornament on Christmas day, but there's an equal number of layouts on which you flat-out stink. Go ahead and fess up.

We all have those specially blessed courses that kick us up one hillside and down the other.

At the top of that long and ignominious list for me is Spyglass Hill Golf Course on California's Monterey Peninsula. So help me, I love it, but it chews me up and spits me into the Pacific breeze like so many spent pine needles. That I can count on. And you know what? I keep going back.

A case of golfer's masochism? Hardly. Spyglass is a trip that not even shooting in the high 90s is going to spoil. How could anyone stay mad when inside the near-pearly gates of Pebble Beach? It's like playing golf in heaven, except that the angels won't help you make par. In fact, they're wrenching their cherubic little faces into painful twists.

My most recent pilgrimage to Spyglass came as my wife and I were celebrating our seventh wedding anniversary. The plan was to splurge big-time: ensconce at the ultraluxurious Casa Palmero, dine at Club XIX (one of the best restaurants on the Monterey Peninsula), and play Spyglass Hill. What's not to love about that?

> We all have those specially blessed courses that kick us up one hillside and down the other.

Well, "love" is probably the wrong word to describe my relationship with Spyglass. "Adversarial?" No, that would imply I'm able to counterattack. "Subservient?" That's more like it: Spyglass Hill is the master; I'm the devoted slave with club in hand who keeps coming back for more. Spyglass is one of Robert Trent Jones Sr.'s best designs, nestled within the dunes and pine trees above that magnificent coastline. But let mine be the voice of warning: It is a beast—a beautiful, and thoroughly nasty, test of golf.

I once interviewed Frank Thacker, who was the head professional at Spyglass from the day the course opened in 1966 through 1976. Thacker recounted to me the first time the Crosby (now the AT&T Pebble Beach National Pro-Am) was played on the layout, less than a year after the course opened. "You talk about a rough, raw, tough course—that was it," he said. "I don't think a course has ever been more cursed than that one was. After that tournament, they remodeled six greens because the slopes were so severe. Arnold Palmer four-putted the 8th green . . . even putted off the green once. And Jack Nicklaus putted into the water on 14! You want to get some people screaming, that's all you need. But I'll tell you this, too: The more difficult the course was by reputation, the more people wanted to come give it a shot."

Golfers are still coming to take their shot at Spyglass more than four decades later. Like gunslingers of the Old West, we are always trying to be king or queen of the hill—in this case, Spyglass Hill. (Of course, like me, most of these golfers end up on Boot Hill.) The master may whip me each and every time, but—obviously I was wrong that masochism doesn't come into play—I can't wait until next time!

PART VI

Tales From the Tour

The Thrill of Victory—Well, Almost

I recently came as close as I'll ever come to winning a professional golf tournament—the LPGA's Office Depot Championship at Trump National Golf Club Los Angeles. What a thrill! Actually, I wasn't really competing in the field. But my Wednesday pro-am playing partner, Hee-Won Han, ended up winning, and I'd like to think I had a wee bit to do with it.

Well, maybe not that much to do with it, since she outdrove me all day long and hit greens where I was a mile wide. But on the putting surface, that's where I may have helped. Though now that I think about it—no, not there either. The other two gents in our foursome were sinking putts with great regularity, however, and maybe Hee-Won took note of their proficiency. Me? I didn't contribute much to the team scramble, except some good humor.

I'd like to think maybe that was enough to keep Hee-Won loose for the ensuing few days of tournament play. Did she stand over a critical 15-foot curler for birdie and think to herself, "What would George say? Man, was he funny!" No. But consider that our team that Wednesday finished at 12 under par, which is the exact same score she carded in the 54 holes of regulation. Our success must have provided some inspiration, right? Maybe some kind of harmonic convergence centered on the number 12?

I must admit, I did not know much about Hee-Won before we teed it up together, but by the end of the tournament, when she had secured a 2-stroke victory over Soo-Yun Kang and a victor's check for $195,000, I was a big fan. During the pro-am event, she had been a friendly playing companion with an inspirational swing. Her drives were long and most of the time perfectly placed. Far from being distant and preoccupied, as some of the PGA Tour players can be on pro-am day, Hee-Won and the rest of the LPGA players I encountered engaged (laughed at?) us amateur hackers, participated freely in pleasant conversation, and appeared to have a grand time outdriving, outputting, and generally whipping up on us guys.

> **Hee-Won and the rest of the LPGA players . . . participated freely in pleasant conversation, and appeared to have a grand time outdriving, outputting, and generally whipping up on us guys.**

Hee-Won, who joined the LPGA in 2001 and was that year's Louise Suggs Rolex Rookie of the Year, was born in Seoul, Korea, and now has a home in San Diego. In this regard, she typifies the new face of the LPGA Tour. Like their brethren on the PGA Tour, LPGA players come from every corner of the globe. "It's like a United Nations out there," then-newly-seated LPGA Commissioner Carolyn Bivens commented.

Proving Bivens' point, 14 of the top 20 finishers at the Office Depot Championship that week were foreign-born, including players from Sweden, Australia, Columbia, France, Scotland, and Korea, which by itself accounted for 7 top finishers—more than any other nation. To further punctuate the impact that Korean players have had on professional golf, Hee-Won's countryman K.J. Choi won the PGA's Chrysler Classic of Greensboro during the same week.

With such international participation, maybe golf's professional tours could assist the United Nations, solving international disputes on the fairways instead of in the contentious political arena of the United Nations Headquarters. Wouldn't it be a better world if conflicts were resolved on a golf course instead of a battlefield? United States to North Korea: "We'll allow your nuclear reactors without comment if you win the match; if we win, shut 'em down." Now that's civil. On a golf course, winning doesn't take guns; it takes birdies.

There is no denying that golf is an international game; in fact, we've known that for some time now. What strikes me as even more inspiring is the fact that—around the world, cheering on that elite flight of touring professionals—are millions of regular, everyday players like you and me, men and women whose drives rocket this way and that, who can't hit a green to save their lives, and who marvel at the skills of players like Hee-Won Han.

For me, it was one of the best days I've ever had on a golf course. And though I may not have contributed much to her win, I sure had a great time rooting her on. The PGA Tour slogan is "These Guys Are Good." If you ask me, in many ways the women are better.

CHAPTER 33

A Babe in Mastersland

The Masters Tournament is considered by many in the United States to be the true opening of the golf season. This sentiment is more widely held in the North and East, of course, where only lunatics and members of the Polar Bear Club venture onto a golf course prior to April. But—groundhogs notwithstanding—the Masters signals the beginning of spring for golfers. The birds start chirping in the trees, the azaleas bloom bright pink, and the ground thaws, meaning chiefly that it won't hurt so bad when you fat your 5 iron into the ground 6 inches behind the ball. Tiger Woods will probably have earned his first couple million of the year already in California and Florida, but it's all a tune-up for the Masters, the first major of the year and the first big gathering of the best players in the world.

Working people across the land celebrate the Masters because it is one of the most popular events of the office pool season (ranking right up there with the Super Bowl and March Madness), and things can get a little boring with nothing to do all day but your job. Heck, what kind of work environment is that? We experts, on the other hand, relish the Masters as an opportunity to make fools of ourselves by offering predictions and picking winners. "There's nothing like picking winners to turn experts into nonexperts fast," the late golf writer Dick Taylor used to say.

Back in his heyday, Taylor would pick only one player to win every tournament—Jack Nicklaus—sagely pointing out that it made no sense to predict that anyone but the best player in the world would prevail. If he were alive today, I'm sure Taylor would say the same about Woods. But in a pool, only one person gets lucky enough to pick Tiger. After that, it's a matter of studied talent evaluation, deep analysis, and (mostly) dumb luck.

One magazine I worked for would rent a house in Augusta each year, and a number of us would go up for the proceedings. Sitting around the kitchen table on the Wednesday night of tournament week, we'd take our picks in the pool. Being given to serious investigative reporting, my main contribution to this hallowed ritual was to come up with the roots of each golfer's surname after he was picked. Let me share some of my findings:

> We experts . . . relish the Masters as an opportunity to make fools of ourselves by offering predictions and picking winners.

- Tiger *Woods*—surname derived from a course hazard
- Brad *Faxon*—derived from office equipment
- Ernie *Els*—named after a slimy sea creature
- Howard *Twitty*—named after a big yellow cartoon character
- Mark Mc*Cumber*—named after a long, green vegetable
- Charles *Coody*—named after an imaginary childhood infirmity
- Ian *Woos*nam—derived from the effects of alcohol
- Brett *Ogle*—named after a dirty old man
- Curtis *Strange*—obviously, appropriately named
- *Duffy Waldorf*—derived from upscale canvas suitcase line
- Steve *Pate*—named after chopped goose liver
- Fred *Couples*—the best golfer name (co-winner)
- Davis *Love III*—the best golfer name (co-winner)

Unfortunately, aside from having a little fun with the names, my role in the pool was strictly that of financial contributor—though giving should never be underestimated. I've never picked an actual winner, and my selections usually don't even make the cut. Clearly, my picks alone prove Mr. Taylor's point about becoming a nonexpert in a hurry.

My first pilgrimage to the Masters was in 1993. I was a babe in Mastersland. The only time I've had a bigger thrill was at the Monterey Jazz Festival when I met Dizzy Gillespie. Diz was softly blowing his horn backstage and I was a lifelong fan. He wasn't scheduled to go on until the following day, so I asked him, "Diz . . . you on today?" He looked up and gave me a friendly growl, "Yeah man. Whaddya wanna hear?" "'Tunisia,' of course." He played it.

This was in my life BG (before golf). Now, with Arnie still among us, Diz playing his bent horn to the angels, and me in the midst of my golfing era, I have an additional set of heroes. Maybe Arnie can't hit a high C on trumpet, but Diz could never hit a high draw on the golf course.

Like the Monterey Jazz Festival, the Masters is a party. People come year after year to stand under the Big Oak Tree outside the clubhouse, visit with each other, and watch the golfers come off the course. If you hang around long enough, you'll meet a Who's Who of the golf business, because sooner or later (usually sooner, since it's where the drinks are) they all gather here.

On the other hand, I didn't meet a single soul who picked Bernhard Langer to win, as he did that first year I went. He was certainly a long shot around our kitchen table. But then again, we're the experts. We enjoy being wrong.

CHAPTER 34

A Primer on Golf Fashion

Barefoot golf is a time-honored tradition in Hawaii, and old photographs from sometime around the 1890s show members of the Hawaiian royal family shoeless on the golf course. I've tried it and can vouch for its great appeal. The warm grass feels spongy and cool as it tickles your feet, and if your golf ball lands in a bunker it's a totally sensual experience having the sand squirm up between your toes. It made me aim for the traps!

On the flip side of that equation, I once played golf with a guy from Tennessee (east Tennessee, for those of you who are sensitive about it) who showed up at the tee box in shorts and cowboy boots equipped with golf cleats. He was a very happy guy—perhaps a little too happy—who delighted in the admonishing looks his getup elicited. Like comedian Bill Murray, whose costumes are part of the entertainment, my friend from Tennessee was "just funnin'," as he put it, in that sweet-as-syrup accent that people from Tennessee have.

> In between barefoot golf and spiked cowboy boots, one finds all manner of shoe fashions on the golf course.

In between barefoot golf and spiked cowboy boots, one finds all manner of shoe fashions on the golf course. Some you might even wish to try (shoes that breathe or display school colors), while others are rather questionable (flip-flops). But I suppose the same can be said of all golf fashion.

Back in the early days of the game, golfers looked dapper. Paintings and old black-and-white photos of tournaments and course scenes show that the golfers were stately looking men, dressed to the nines, often hitting the links in tweed coats and ties, or knickers and knee-high socks.

In the 1920s and '30s, Bobby Jones, Gene Sarazen, and Walter Hagen set the tone, sporting crisp white shirts with starched collars, bow ties, snazzy sweaters, and fancy leather shoes. Even through the '40s and '50s, golfers could be counted on for spot-on fashion. Two fine examples were Byron Nelson and Ben Hogan. Nelson was more of a throwback to the formal look, while Hogan ushered in an era of relaxed, yet totally spiffy, country club fashions, a look advanced by the young Arnold Palmer.

Then in the '60s and '70s, all hell broke loose in golf fashion. With the notable exception of Gary Player, who, like Johnny Cash, dressed all in black, fashion in this era gave us a reputation as bad—very bad—dressers, and it's a tag we carry to this day.

The worst offender, unfortunately, was also one of the highest-profile players: Johnny Miller. Not that he was alone in his lack of taste—Miller's contemporary Doug Sanders was known as the "Peacock of the Fairways" for his unsightly outfits—but Miller set the bar high with his hideously checked pants, thick white belts, neon sweaters, and other attire we can all look back on and thank our lucky stars we weren't photographed wearing. (Not that we didn't wear them.)

Thankfully, today's pros are, for the most part, fashion plates. In the well-dressed and trendy camp is Tiger Woods, always impeccably outfitted and proudly logoed. In the questionable camp are Jesper Parnevik, the effervescent Swede whose fashions—bright colors (limes, pinks), disturbing patterns, skin-tight slacks, upturned cap bill—are more often the topic of conversation than is his golf game; Sergio Garcia, who often wears orange and plum together (or some such combination that crosses my eyes on sight); Ian Poulter, who often plays in his rooster hair and costume; and Camilo Villegas, who you'd swear went to Johnny Miller's yard sale.

I offer the following from a story on www.anyonefortee.com, wherein "leading British eye surgeon Professor Sir Ian Ball" was quoted as saying, "I'm very worried about Ian Poulter. He'll never make it to the top as long as keeps wearing those clothes. Of course, he often wears sunglasses for protection, so that may help a little. Then look at Johnny Miller back in the '70s. A brilliant player in his early career, but when the fashion bug caught up with him, he was never the same again. You just can't play when your brain is confused by excessive stimuli.

"Jesper Parnevik is another example. The more eccentric his dress, the worse he plays. Not to mention the effect it has on his playing partners. Just ask Mark Roe about that disqualification in the 2003 Open. He's a fine professional, but he managed to sign the wrong scorecard. Only a man suffering severe disorientation would do that—it was clearly down to Jesper's trousers."*

On the other hand, there are those who feel that golf could use more players like Poulter, Garcia, and Villegas, and who wish that Parnevik were but the tip of the wild-and-crazy fashion iceberg. One such person is Loudmouth Golf founder Scott Woodworth, whose stated goal is a much (and I mean much) brighter golf future: "We all grew up watching Johnny Miller in his shocking red pants and white belt, and Jack Nicklaus in his plaid polyester Sansabelts. But when the time came for us to golf decades later, what sartorial choices were we given?"**

The fashions that Woodworth has created cannot be described in words, no matter how much I'd like to tell you about them. They are unbelievable. If I tried to paint a picture for you of his eye-popping disco ball trousers, his lime and forest green argyles, or his brazen barcode stripes, I'd never do them justice. So go try Google; you really do have to see these with your own eyes.

Meanwhile, I'll be out shopping for cleated motorcycle racing boots and having my local seamstress sew AstroTurf to the seat of my zebra-striped lederhosen. I'm determined to set the next fashion trend in motion.

---

* Adapted, by permission, from Duffersgolf Ltd., 2005, *Loud trouser warning must not fall on deaf ears!* [Online]. Available: http://www.anyonefortee.com/News/Trouserwatch1.html [June 6, 2008].
** Source: Loudmouth Golf, www.loudmouthgolf.com

How to Host a U.S. Open

Many of us hang out every weekend in loose-knit groups of 20 or 30 golfers who enjoy playing together. We call ourselves things like the Salinas Hackers, the Montclair Chili-Dippers, the Southside Slicers, and so on. I'm a dues-paying member of the Penmar-by-the-Sea Type-Os, a group of writers and media flacks like me. Most of these stalwarts of American golf play at cheap courses, looking to pay $30 to $50 per head per round. Most of us have home courses that get the bulk of our group's play, but every fourth weekend or so, we like to move around for variety.

The United States Golf Association (USGA), which puts golfers into various categories, calls such groups "Member Clubs Without Real Estate." And if you can believe our good fortune, USGA rules permit clubs like ours to apply to host a U.S. Open. All we need is the consent of our home course and—voilà!—we're on our way to hosting the most prestigious tournament in the land.

I say let's host the U.S. Open at Penmar-by-the-Sea, where the Type-Os hold forth. And why not? The USGA wants to hold the Open more often at public facilities, as evidenced by the recent choices of Torrey Pines (2008) and Bethpage Black (2002 and 2009), either of which would qualify as an "Everygolfer's" paradise. So does our little Penmar. Haven't we had our fill of seeing the Open at Congressional Country Club, Shinnecock Hills, Oakmont, and the like—private courses that most golfers in the country couldn't get on if a rich uncle were a member? I say hooray to the USGA for holding the U.S. Open at Hacker's Corner, USA. Let's hold more at facilities exactly like that.

Bethpage Black is a perfect example. Owned by the state of New York, the course is swamped every weekend by a representative array of golfers. Foursomes get in the "car line" up to 24 hours in advance to try to secure one of the six foursome slots. It's fun, and it feels more like the parking lot at your average football stadium on a Sunday morning than a heretofore reserved and refined gentleman's country club. Car line parties at Bethpage feature tailgate barbecues, "keggers," and folks who loudly whoop it up until they fall asleep in their cars.

> I say hooray to the USGA for holding the U.S. Open at Hacker's Corner, USA. Let's hold more at facilities exactly like that.

The next morning, tee time tickets are handed out at 5 a.m. Tee times range from 8 a.m. to 9 a.m., giving these stiff, cold warriors a chance to guzzle some coffee, wash their faces, wipe their noses on their sleeves, and maybe get some breakfast. Then they go out and attempt to play well on one of the most challenging courses they'll ever play. A sign near the 1st tee even warns them to turn back if they are not experienced. But that would be like getting to the base of Mount Everest and deciding to turn back because a sign says that people die up there. What do you think we came here for, high tea? Of course people die up here; otherwise, we'd be playing Tiddlywinks.

So you adjust the Velcro on your golf glove, tie your FootJoys a little tighter, and head toward your golfing demise with determination. It may take one hole. It may take three. But Bethpage Black will conquer you, just as surely as you rise in the morning and brush the fur off your teeth.

I'm not advocating here that the pros go through what the rest of us have to go through to get a tee time at a popular public facility, although it might be funny to see them chauffeured from their private jets to the golf course in a Geo Metro in which they also have to sleep. "Right here, Mr. Mickelson, is the lever that will lower your seat back to a perfectly uncomfortable position. And don't worry too much about the excruciating pain in your back tomorrow morning from the cramped quarters and freezing cold; 15 to 20 Extra-Strength Tylenols should help."

No, what I'm advocating is a continuation of the USGA's bravery in taking the Open to public facilities. Several positive things happen. First, the course in question receives the best attention: the grasses improve, as do the putting surfaces, and probably the clubhouse too. But the more important element is that a course on which you and I can play anytime gets tested by the world's best players. We can relate to their successes and miseries.

We know what happens when you come up short here or go right there. We've all tried to hit over that tree or reach that par 5 in two. We may not know what it's like to shoot in the 60s for 4 days, but we sure can appreciate what it takes for the best players in the world to shoot 30 strokes per day better than we do on our own home course.

The logistics may not support my request for a U.S. Open on Penmar-by-the-Sea, a nine-hole track with barely enough parking slots for 50 cars. Where exactly would the 55,000 people, the hospitality and merchandise tents, and the concession stands go? But *your* home course, my friend, might be perfect.

So keep your heads high, hackers of the world. Next time the U.S. Open comes to your neck of the woods, perhaps it won't be at that fancy-dancy club on the hill for the hundredth time. Perhaps, at last, it will be on the home turf of the Montclair Chili-Dippers, the Southside Slicers, or (maybe they could go around our nine-hole layout twice) the Penmar Type-Os. At least we can hope.

CHAPTER 36

Looking Down
at the Grass

Golf commentators have long complained—mostly in private for fear of being kicked out of the fraternity—about today's cardboard-cutout tour pros, who dare not stray one iota from the straight-and-narrow behavior guidelines prescribed by the PGA Tour, whose interviews are so much predictable blather, and whose personalities are as exciting as drying house paint. Once in a while, we get a John Daly, a boozing, tempestuous, go-for-broke kind of player who is as colorful and troubled as he is talented, and we fixate on his every move.

The PGA Tour used to be full of such characters! Guys like Jimmy Demaret, who upon being told of his 9 a.m. starting time at the Crosby Clambake remarked, "9 a.m.? I don't even puke before 10!" And Walter Hagen, who showed up on the 1st tee at the British Open one year in a formal tuxedo, having come to the course in a rented limo directly from a night of drinking and carrying on. Or "Champagne Tony" Lema, a vivacious, larger-than-life personality who would celebrate his victories by cracking a few bottles of bubbly with his pals in the press room.

Pals in the pressroom? Nowadays, that's unheard of. Golf has become so dominated by big money and corporate sponsorships, and the media so obsessed with overblown sensationalism, that the relationship between players and the golf press is mostly functional, often mundane, and frequently bordering on boring.

Here's how it usually goes in the media room:

> **New York Times:** Tiger, can you give details of the eagle you made on 15?
>
> **Tiger:** 3 wood and 5 wood and a putt from about 8 feet.

Snore. Here's how we'd like to see it go:

> **New York Times:** Tiger, what happened on 15, when you skanked your 3 wood so far right and behind that boulder, and the PGA Tour official ruled that it was a moveable object? How many spectators did it take to help move that mass of granite so you could hit 5 wood to the green?
>
> **Tiger:** Thanks for asking, Larry. Say, is that a raccoon sitting on your head? Oh, that's your hair!

Back in the day—from the 1920s to the 1960s—the players were very colorful. I'm talking about guys like Demaret, Sam Snead, Chi Chi Rodriguez, and Lee Trevino. The things they'd say, often off the cuff, would crack you up. Trevino, still a master of the hilarious, once replied, when interviewed about how he played on a particular day, "I'm not saying my golf game went bad, but if I grew tomatoes, they'd come up sliced."

Then there's this Trevino gem: "Columbus went around the world in 1492. That isn't a lot of strokes when you consider the course." In another classic, Trevino once said of his own play, "My swing is so bad I look like a caveman killing his lunch." And finally, the Merry Mex reminds us, "If you're caught on a golf course during a storm and are afraid of lightning, hold up a 1 iron. Not even God can hit a 1 iron." Priceless. In a similar spirit of irreverence, the irrepressible Chi Chi Rodriguez once confessed, "The first time I played the Masters, I was so nervous I drank a bottle of rum before I teed off. I shot the happiest 83 of my life."

In an April 2000 *Golf Digest* feature on Demaret, Nick Seitz told this story: "The extroverted Demaret kidded the introverted [Ben] Hogan as pithily as he kidded everybody else, and Hogan relished it. One day Demaret walked into a clubhouse dining room, saw Hogan eating at a table by himself, and piped: 'Hey, look, there's Ben Hogan sitting with all his friends.'" It was also Demaret who gave the world this little beauty: "Golf and sex are the only things you can enjoy without being good at them."

Another of my favorite golf quotes of all time is attributed to the British golfer and sportsman Horace G. Hutchinson: "If profanity had an influence on the flight of the ball, the game of golf would be played far better than it is." Convinced that 90 percent of the game is mental, the great American champion Bobby Jones once declared, "Golf is a game that is played on a five-inch course—the distance between your ears." Modern champion Ben Crenshaw concurred, "I'm about five inches from being an outstanding golfer. That's the distance my left ear is from my right." Four-time major winner Ray Floyd opined, "They call it golf because all of the other four-letter words were taken."

Then there was Slammin' Sammy Snead, who holds the PGA Tour record for most career victories with 82 (though many expect Tiger will eventually best that mark). When asked about a course he was playing, he had this to say: "These greens are so fast I have to hold my putter over the ball and hit it with the shadow." Here's more Snead: "The fairways were so narrow you had to walk down them single file" and "Nobody asked how you looked, just what you shot." I was lucky enough once to meet the legendary Snead in person, over chocolate milk shakes. What a hoot!

Known for his prodigious drives and dead-on putting, Sam was also one of the most beloved players ever to grace the game.

He was infamous early in his career for playing tournaments barefoot, and later was all but inseparable from his trademark straw hat. He was renowned for his folksy, homespun humor and easygoing ways—traits not at all uncommon in the deep Allegheny Mountains of Virginia where he lived his entire life and where we met.

I was in Hot Springs, Virginia, Sam's hometown—an area he described as having "valleys so narrow that the dogs have to wag their tails up and down"—and had just finished playing 18 holes on the Homestead Resort's Lower Cascades Course. Sitting down to grab a bite in the clubhouse, I noticed Snead a few tables away, sitting by himself, about to order as well. Wishing only to shake the great man's hand and say hello, I went over. "I don't want to bother you," I said, "but I just wanted to say hello. I've always been a big fan of yours." He lit up. "Please, sit," he said, gracious as only a country gentleman can be. "I've just come from the dentist and I'm starving, but can't have any solid food. Join me. You'll love the chocolate milk shakes here." A chocolate milk shake with Sam Snead? Who could say no to that?

I have a signed, hardback edition of his book *The Education of a Golfer* and have read it cover to cover countless times. In it, Snead reveals the secrets of his flawless swing, which was the envy of every player of his day. Onetime USGA president William Campbell once remarked, "He was the best natural player ever. He had the eye of an eagle, the grace of a leopard, and the strength of a lion." John Schlee, 1973 U.S. Open runner-up (to Johnny Miller) said, "Watching Sam Snead practice hitting golf balls is like watching a fish practice swimming." Snead made the cut that year at 61 years of age (setting a still-unbroken record as the oldest player to make the cut in a U.S. Open), and he finished tied for 29th.

As I sat down, I wanted to ask him everything at once: about his trying early days on Tour; what it took to persevere, to succeed; his swing; his approach to the game. But Sam wanted to talk about milk shakes and dentists. Turned out we both despised dentists and loved milk shakes! We pondered if one had a direct effect on the other. He finally asked about my game. Was I a decent player? "One day, not too bad. The next day, ouch," I told him. "Know what you mean," he said. "That's golf. Keep it in perspective; have fun. When you start crying on your own shoulder, you're in trouble." We laughed a while, he told some more stories, we drank our milk shakes.

As he got up to leave, I wished him good luck and good health. "Same to you, young man," he said. "As you get older, you take heart in remembering what Arnold Palmer said: 'It's far better to be looking down at the grass than looking up at the grass.'" Amen to that. And to all the colorful players who have walked the fairways of golf.

Whistling While You Work

I used to work with a lovely young woman I called Songbird. That's because she'd sit at her desk and whistle while she worked. It was such a pleasant experience to walk past and hear her idle whistling; it brightened the day. She sounded just like a songbird in the branches of a tree.

Golfers whistle for a different reason: to relieve pressure. But it is still a pleasant thing to hear. I used to enjoy watching PGA Tour professional Mark McCumber, for example, whistle his way to victory. I recall once watching him and Fuzzy Zoeller tee off together in a playoff at the 1994 Tour Championship at the Olympic Club in San Francisco. The musical possibilities were infinite because both were whistlers, and if the playoff had lasted more than one hole I was looking forward to seeing them march up and down the fairways of that grand old golf course whistling, say, the refrain from *The Bridge on the River Kwai*.

If you ask me, that's the way golf should be approached. I've played rounds with enough swearers and club throwers to last a lifetime. Well, I'll be honest: On occasion, I've even been a swearer and club thrower. So I understand. Golf can be frustrating and nerve-racking, particularly if you're playing for big bucks as McCumber and Zoeller were. But they whistled, and both are winners. Nowadays, they play the occasional tournament on the Champions Tour, and both are still whistling away.

Even as McCumber and Zoeller embodied serenity on that final day in San Francisco, Bill Glasson was in a different world. At the time, he was a 12-year PGA Tour veteran with six career victories under his belt, including that year's Phoenix Open, which helped vault him into the Tour Championship. But on this particular day, Glasson parlayed a 3-day tournament lead into a series of mis-hit shots that caused him to drop down the leaderboard and eventually lose the championship. The more bad shots he hit, the more uptight he got. You could see it in his play and in the tightening muscles of his face. My suggestion to Bill: Start whistling.

> I've played rounds with enough swearers and club throwers to last a lifetime.

A more poignant contrast involves the previous year's Tour Championship, also held at the Olympic Club, when Greg Norman needed only par to force a playoff on Sunday afternoon. Instead he got himself into the same treacherous position above the 18th pin that McCumber would grapple with a year later. A clearly uptight Norman chipped way past the hole, bogeyed, and handed the trophy to a waiting Jim Gallagher Jr.

Granted, that position above the hole looks impossible. A shoebox probably wouldn't stop rolling there, much less a golf ball. Norman couldn't do it, and McCumber couldn't do it. But the point here is not to criticize shoeboxes, Norman, or Glasson; it is to focus on whistling.

Or how about singing? I wouldn't mind hearing Craig Stadler do an aria from *The Barber of Seville* before he teed off, particularly if he was sporting his scruffy, rough-and-tumble look that day. Or John Daly belting out "All You Need Is Love" as he lined up a putt. But perhaps whistling is a better idea. You don't need to carry a tune to whistle. In fact, you don't really even need to know a tune to whistle. As Lauren Bacall advised Humphrey Bogart in *To Have and Have Not*, "You know how to whistle, don't you? Just put your lips together and blow."

Not everyone, of course, appreciates whistling (or cigar smoke, for that matter) in their foursome. The golf writer David Wood even published an item titled "The Original Rules of Golf Revisited," in which one maxim states, "Any golfer caught whistling in an irritating manner while golfing (and in recorded history the only non-irritating whistling is the opening theme of the *Andy Griffith Show*) shall lose the use of their putter and driver for the remainder of their golfing life. Remember, if the golf gods wanted you to whistle, they would have given you wings and a beak."

McCumber and Zoeller would take exception, and so would I. When a bad round might cost them a couple hundred thousand dollars—which is the difference between first and second place—any shrink worth his salt would give the same advice: Relax, put a song in your head, and whistle. Do whatever it takes. Grinders expect bad things to happen; whistlers expect good. Plus, like a teapot, you're letting off steam.

So if it helps, go ahead and whistle, Mark and Fuzzy. I've even become a whistler myself, combining idle day-brightening with a relief of pressure, much like the fellow in John Dryden's poem, who "trudged along, unknowing what he sought / And whistled as he went for want of thought."

WHACK!

Bada-Bing—A Proposal to Improve the AT&T Pebble Beach National Pro-Am by Changing That Way-Too-Long Name and Bringing Back the Spirit of Bing Crosby

Everybody loves Raymond but me. I hate Raymond. Well, it's not that I hate Ray Romano, star of the long-running CBS sitcom *Everybody Loves Raymond*, since I don't really hate anybody. But I sure do get tired of watching his lousy golf game on the AT&T Pebble Beach National Pro-Am (what a mouthful!) broadcast *every* year. It's not just him. I'm tired of watching all those big shots out there compiling cumulus-high scores while their accompanying professional politely looks on. Maybe Scott Simpson enjoys playing with Bill Murray— who wouldn't? But three days of Neil Young, Huey Lewis, or Kevin Costner flubbing around the golf course is too darn much.

> I'm tired of watching all those big shots out there compiling cumulus-high scores.

Romano has an 18 handicap. Kevin James, of CBS' *The King of Queens*, another show I never watched, also sports an 18 handicap. I've played with funnier guys at my local muni; what's more, they play better golf than these stars do. At $40 a day for a ticket to the AT&T Pebble Beach National Pro-Am, my buddies Bobby "Worm Burner" and "Slice of" Eric are a better deal, too. And at least I get some exercise.

I will admit there are a few guys I would pay to watch. Murray (with a reported 13.4 handicap) is at the top of the list. Kenny G, sure. He has a decent swing, both on the course and with his sax. And Craig T. Nelson, whose television credits include *The District* and *Coach*, is not only a credible actor but also a good stick whose handicap hovers around 5. But Kevin Costner? Nada. His 12-plus handicap plays more like a 36, and his flops aren't limited to the golf course. Costner ain't on my list of guys I'd pay to watch. Neil Young? Sorry, old pal. Rust may never sleep on your guitar, but your golf game needs lubrication.

> I've played with funnier guys at my local muni; what's more, they play better golf than these stars do.

I know, I know, the celebrity thing is tradition at Pebble, and it's the reason Bing started the tournament in the first place. And it raises good money for many charitable causes in the area. But every PGA Tour event raises money for good causes. It's just that all the other events manage to keep the pro-am element in perspective by devoting one day, generally Tuesday or Wednesday, to the corporate bosses and celebrity hacks, as opposed to every single darn day at Pebble.

Granted, not every tournament gets such a turnout of movie and television stars and musicians. And CBS obviously uses the tournament to hype its shows and stars for the February "sweeps," which determine network advertising prices for the upcoming period. But am I the only one who has reached celebrity overload? Minute-by-minute coverage of George Lopez hacking out of the ice plant just kinda hits my "SHUT UP ALREADY!" button.

Have we gone completely bonkers with celebrity coverage? Have you looked at a supermarket checkout rack recently? I've had enough of the Brad Pitt, Angelina Jolie, Britney Spears, and Lindsay Lohan headlines. Who cares? (If you answered "I do" to this question, please skip to the next chapter, since the balance of this one may be offensive to you.) I say we get it all out at once on the golf course and be done: Brad versus Brit, Angelina versus Lindsay, 18 holes, match play. Losers get no more media

> Losers get no more media coverage for the rest of their lives, even if they get married or divorced, crash cars, enter rehab, or adopt African babies.

coverage for the rest of their lives, even if they get married or divorced, crash cars, enter rehab, or adopt African babies.

And even though Bing Crosby might be spinning in his grave by now, let's settle a few other things while we're at it. How about Bruce Willis versus Ashton Kutcher for Demi Moore's affection; Adam Sandler versus Bill Murray in clown suits for the title "Funniest Golfer"; and reformed drug addicts Rush Limbaugh and David Crosby facing off in prison jumpsuits (just for fun)? CBS can broadcast the whole thing as a *Survivor* episode. Bada-bing!

And here's a bright idea. Let's pit Arnold Schwarzenegger against Martin Sheen—nationally televised—with all proceeds from broadcast rights and advertising going to pay down the national debt. They would have to play straight up, because even though Sheen carries a reported 16 handicap, versus the Governator's 24, we all know the Republican expertise in raising funds is superior, so let's call them even.

And if we really want to attract a larger audience, we should also include the women. Imagine the television appeal of Catherine Zeta-Jones (with her reported 20 handicap) versus Anna Kournikova (who cares what her handicap is?). Now that's a good use of celebrity golf. How about it, Mr. Eastwood? Sure, you and I have met only once, way back when you were mayor of Carmel and both of us were bellied up to the bar at Club XIX with soup on our ties, but will you give this stuff some thought? As chairman of the Monterey Peninsula Foundation, the organization that calls the shots on this type of thing, you have some pull. No? I didn't think so. Dribbled clam chowder goes only so far.

CBS, how about you? Can you fellas at least twirl the cameras in the direction of some of the real golfers once in a while this year? With players like Jason Gore,

CBS, how about you? Can you fellas at least twirl the cameras in the direction of some of the real golfers once in a while this year?

Matt Kuchar, Phil Mickelson, and that guy named Tiger, there may be some action to cover away from the celebrity couch. And if you can bring yourselves to do this, then maybe you can help me out with the rest of my wish list:

George's Wish List for the AT&T Pebble Beach National Pro-Am

1. I wish it was still called "The Crosby" or "The Clambake," because saying "AT&T Pebble Beach National Pro-Am" is a load.
2. I wish they still had a clambake.
3. Let's include two days of celebrity golf, then get down to professional golf.
4. People in the gallery should be allowed to bring their cameras again. Why have celebrities if you can't take photos of the shenanigans?
5. I wish Jack Lemmon were still with us.
6. I wish Jack Lemmon had made the cut, just once.
7. Cut back the celebs to those with a 10 handicap or better.
8. New title proposal 1: If they're going to persist in calling it the AT&T Pebble Beach National Pro-Am, I wish they would add "(Man, That's a Mouthful!)" to the title, too. What's a few more words?

9. New title proposal 2: If you don't like proposal 1, then let's call it the "AT&T Pebble Beach Formerly the Crosby National Celebrity CBS Sweeps Tournament With Oh Yeah Some PGA Tour Professionals Too."

10. I wish they'd let me in the press room, but I guess my book just isn't important enough for them.

The 19th Hole

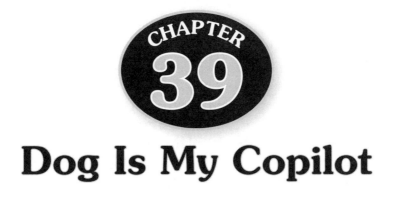

CHAPTER 39

Dog Is My Copilot

I'm a dog guy. In our home, we have no kids and two pooches, who travel with us just about everywhere. These two characters are welcome at the most elegant hotels. They dine with us on the decks of nice restaurants and even accompany us into stores and onto airplanes. Meet Strutter and Arielle, an Italian greyhound and a whippet, respectively. Why are they not welcome on golf courses? What is it that a golf course is trying to protect that the Ritz-Carlton isn't? The carpet?

Count me in as a full, dues-paying member of the first golf course in the United States that allows us houndspeople to bring our best friends along on the hunt for birdies. I might even contemplate a run for president of the club. During my administration, Snoozing Pup Golf Links will be an innovative place, and it is to be hoped that other courses around the country would take note and change their anti-pooch policies.

> Count me in as a full, dues-paying member of the first golf course in the United States that allows us houndspeople to bring our best friends along on the hunt for birdies.

For example, the golf carts at Snoozing Pup would come equipped with water bowls, tasty treats, and poopie pickup bags. Each cart would also have a retractable leash in the rear so the pup can get some exercise as we drive to our golf ball. We'd have comfy beds installed where those useless wire baskets now take up space, and just imagine your dog's joy at being asked to retrieve your ball from a water hazard!

We could also institute training classes in sniffing out golf balls lost in the woods, as apparently a certain J.D. Foot did in Pinehurst, North Carolina, in 1909. According to a story in the *New York Times* on March 28, 1909, Mr. Foot, a Native American golfer from the Apawamis tribe, "trained his setters to hunt for golf balls, and during occasional walks he gather[ed] in a pocketful or so without half trying." The story quoted Foot as saying that while it would be impossible to teach some dogs this new trick, "others take to it readily and apparently find keen enjoyment in it." I'm presuming Mr. Foot determined his dog's level of enjoyment when it muttered (ah, so that's where the word *"muttered"* came from!), "Thanks for teaching me this, J.D. Now I'll never be out of work." Or maybe the dog just flashed a big smile.

Additional helpful activities dogs on golf courses could perform include squirrel chasing—keeping those fat little rascals away from your sandwich while you're putting—and goose shooing. Superintendents should be thrilled to have such well-trained help keeping those pesky Canada Geese (and their droppings) off the greens. In fact, I came across one enterprising New Jersey company, Geese Police, that helps hundreds of golf course superintendents across the country "get the flock out," as the company's motto states. Using specially trained border collies—there are five "deputy dogs" in the New Jersey office—the Geese Police "herd and harass, but never harm," the offending geese.*

Even aside from the practical arguments, I'm certain that golfers would enjoy the game more if their furry friends were along for the ride. I can tell you that when I'm having a bad day, nothing cools my jets more than a loving look and a shake of the tail from my two hounds.

It also strikes me as odd that there are so few courses with "dog" in their name. Considering how fond we are of our mangy mutts, wouldn't you think there would be more? The most famous, of course, is Pete Dye's masterwork: Teeth of the Dog,

* Source: Geese Police, www.geesepoliceinc.com

in the Dominican Republic. And readers in northwest Illinois, on the Iowa border, might have played the nine-hole Red Dog Run Golf Course in East Moline. But even at those fine facilities, dogs are not allowed to join in the fun.

There are literally hundreds of courses with some form of "eagle" in their name—Eagle's Landing, Eagle Nest, Double Eagle, Eagle Trace, Golden Eagle Golf & Country Club, to name a few—as well as more than enough "bear" courses to go around: Bear's Best, Bear Trap, Bear Butt . . . OK, I made that last one up, but come on! Enough with the birds and the bears. Who's going to represent for the world's canines? I say let's get them front and center. In addition to Snoozing Pup Golf Links, here are some other unused names: Hound's Hollow Golf Club, Strutting Mutt Links, Squatting Pooch Country Club. Who wouldn't be a member at SPCC?

As far as I can tell, there are few occasions where we hear the word *dog* used in relation to golf. Of course there's a "dogleg left" or "dogleg right" in golf course design. And then there's an expression of frustration that often involves a blown shot or match, such as when Golf Channel commentator Dottie Pepper called the 2007 American Solheim Cup team "choking, freakin' dogs" on live television after the ladies had blown leads in two matches. Similarly, when I miss a 1-foot putt for bogey on any given Sunday, I'll declare myself a "stinking dog." And—rarer for me—when I hit the holy hell out of my driver, someone might remark, "Geez, you really let the Big Dog eat on that one."

Dogs deserve a more respected place in golf. Indeed, if they are truly our best friends—as so many poems, quotations, and songs declare—then they should certainly be welcome in our favorite game. The fact is, we can take our dogs just about anywhere these days and involve them in many sports: hunting, fishing— heck, we've even seen pictures of pooches on surfboards. So listen up, golf courses of the world: Strutter and Arielle can't wait to meet you.

Dew Sweepers, Diehards, and the Dearly Departed

Dew sweepers, dawn patrol, jackrabbits: Call them what you will, there is a group of dedicated—some would call them zany—golfers in the United States who have played 18 holes before you brush your teeth in the morning. These are the guys who have a standing order with their pro shop for the first tee time available on the sheet, and they don't care if the sun is up. Clerks at all-night doughnut shops and 24-hour convenience stores know who they are. They're the guys who come in at 4:30 a.m. looking for the pot of coffee and spouting an all-too-cheery greeting: "Top of the morning to you!" The bleary-eyed, nocturnal clerks stare blankly, but no matter—the golf course awaits.

Every course seems to have its own version of dew sweepers. Some belong to organized groups that capitalize the "D" and hold formal early morning gatherings. Some groups even post photographs on the Web. Golf writer James Dodson wrote a book about the camaraderie he developed by spending a year in the company of one such madcap cluster of men.

Then there are the diehards. These golfers play every day of the year. If they live in the northern climes and their home course is frozen over in the dead of winter, they'll shovel off a patch of hardpan in their backyard and hit orange balls into the snowdrifts.

Either that or they've installed a net in their living room or basement so they can hit balls into it until spring finally comes.

Diehards and dew sweepers have quite a bit in common, even beyond their uncommon zeal. Both groups display such a deep love of the game and for their similarly afflicted colleagues that their spouses might be tempted to refer them to a shrink. "Honey," she says, as your alarm clock goes off at 4 a.m. "Can't we go to Wal-Mart together later this morning?" "Ah sweetums, you know I can't stand the boys up. Who would they get to replace me?" "Why did you sleep in your golf shoes?" she asks, rubbing the sleep out of her eyes. "Would you consider seeing a shrink?" "I'll go to a doctor, all right . . . Dr. Green," you snap back on your way out the door. It's the only appropriate response.

> These golfers play every day of the year. If they live in the northern climes . . . , they'll shovel off a patch of hardpan in their backyard and hit orange balls into the snowdrifts.

The guys who really crack me up, though, are those who will even play through a corpse, like the dearly departed was just another course hazard. Talk about taking the term "diehard" to extremes! "Hey, Joe, do I get a free drop from behind this dead guy?" "I think a dead body is considered a moveable obstruction," Joe says. "Just roll him out of your line." I read stories like this every now and again. I'm innocently thumbing through the newspaper scanning all the political scandals, boardroom collusions, and terror plots when I come across an item of real interest: Some golfer died on the 18th green of a course somewhere in Florida, and all the other foursomes behind him played through before the coroner arrived to cart him away.

Another recent story, found on the Web, involved a 65-year-old golfer who drove his cart off a cliff in California while looking for his lost golf ball. He plunged down a 25-foot embankment and through some bushes, then fell another 60 feet to the highway, where he was pronounced dead by paramedics. What I found most amazing about this item were the comments posted by other golfers. Here's a sampling:

> **OmegaMan II:** Was it worth it? I mean, did he find the golf ball?

> **Dogman66:** Wonder if he was buried in the golf cart?

> **JRios1968:** ProV-1s are pricey, sure, but they're not worth THAT much.

> **Trumandogz:** Thelma & Louise golf course.

> **Llevrok:** Were his golf clubs damaged or are they fine?

> **OmegaMan II:** Honey, let's take up golfing. You drive, I'll walk. Ahem, you know I need the exercise!

Now you have to admit there's something tragicomic about a golfer being so obsessed with a lost golf ball that he drives his cart over a cliff. You can almost picture the *New Yorker* cartoon. But fellas, a guy died here! Let's show a little respect. I've also read about golfers who drove golf carts into ponds and drowned, and about carts that flipped over and crushed the occupants. Then there are stories about golfers being felled by lightning strikes, and of course the great Bing Crosby died of a heart attack on the golf course in Spain. The fact is, studies have shown that golf courses are the fifth most common public place for people to suffer cardiac arrest.

It's dangerous on a golf course!

But nothing I've ever heard tops a story reported in the *New York Times*. An 83-year-old golfer named Peter Sedore scored his 18th career hole-in-one. The shot came on the 129-yard fourth hole at a course called Panorama Village. On the next hole, he collapsed. The octogenarian's son said that there was no other way his father would have wanted to go. Indeed, if you're going to have to check out, I suppose the golf course is not a bad place to be, particularly for us diehards and dew sweepers.

CHAPTER 41

Dweezel and Chuckles Rip Me a Shred Stick

I play a lot of Sunday morning golf as a single. Most of the time I'm paired with fine, upstanding, and wholly decent folk, but every once in a while, I'll get to the 1st tee and find that I've signed up for 18 holes of hell.

Sadly, such was the case last weekend, when I got stuck in a quintet (yes, our local muni sends out fivesomes) with Dweezel and Chuckles. I have no idea what their real names were, which is lucky because I might have tracked them down and had my Uncle Luigi make a house call with his violin case to deliver an offer they couldn't refuse. After the 1st hole, I simply anointed them Dweezel and Chuckles because they were so irritating and I couldn't think of anything more insulting to call them that early in the morning. (If any of you have suggestions on highly creative and well-thought-out insult names, please e-mail them to me so that next time I'll be more prepared.)

How were they irritating? Glad you asked. For starters, they were annoying just to look at. Dweezel wore some kind of black high-top tennis shoes, baggy cargo shorts, and a white t-shirt that read, "Reverse Rip My Shred Stick." He had on a baseball cap that said Hurley, and he wore it cocked ever-so-sideways. Whenever his pal Chuckles hit the ball—usually sideways— Dweezel would say, "Wow, dude. Rad." Surf rat? Maybe. Golf course? Get lost.

Chuckles was only a smidge more refined than his airheaded buddy, sporting a t-shirt that read "Jimmy Eat World Highway 104 Tour 2008." He'd smack his tee ball into the weeds and immediately start digging in the pocket of his pink-and-lime-colored Bermudas for another ball. "Long as I paid my $17 to play," he'd say, "I might as well learn." And before you could furrow your brow and figure out what he could possibly mean by that, he'd hit a second and then a third into the very same weeds.

Finally, on the 3rd tee box, I asked, "Come on, Chuckles, how many balls are you going to hit?" "What, man? I paid my money." The fivesome behind us had already caught up and were glaring at us to get moving. Wanting to avoid a rumble, I tried explaining to Chuckles and Dweezel that the Rules of Golf do not allow for "do-overs," nor for learning the game while 15 angry golfers line up waiting for you to clear the tee. "Wow, dude," in unison. "Rad." I could tell this was going to be one of those days.

> **Wanting to avoid a rumble, I tried explaining . . . that the Rules of Golf do not allow for "do-overs," nor for learning the game while 15 angry golfers line up waiting for you to clear the tee.**

My friend and fellow golf vagabond Joel Zuckerman calls guys like this "freaks along the fairway." In his book *Misfits on the Links*, Zuckerman identifies 40 characters to avoid, many of whom you might recognize from your home course. Among them is Mulligan Man, who, like Chuckles, hits ball after ball after ball until he's happy with his mediocrity, even if doing so clearly rubs everyone else on the golf course the wrong way. Mulligan Men, Zuckerman reminds us, have an all-time favorite saying: "If at first you don't succeed, try, try, try, try, and try again."

Zuckerman also pegs the Boozehound, who has really funny comments about why he's drinking beer so early in the morning on the 1st tee, and the 2nd tee, and the 3rd . . . There's also the Cell Mate, who says he can't stand it when other people talk on cell phones while playing yet spends his the entire round "trying to close a deal" himself, and the Gambler, a complete sandbagger, whose favorite line is, "Maybe we should play for a little something. Just to keep it interesting." Keep it interesting? It would be completely interesting for me if I never got paired with any of you guys.

Other, slightly less irritating characters we've all encountered on golf courses include the Chronic Complainer, who can find fault with any shot he hits, despite the fact that he's on the green in regulation and putting for birdie while everyone else in his group is searching for their golf balls in the woods. "My God, Glen," he'll bitch to himself. "Can't you hit the damn ball? What's wrong with you?" I always want to look at this guy and say, "Glen, shut the hell up before I shove my 2 iron down your piehole and send my Uncle Luigi to your house with his violin case!"

Then there is the guy who decides—usually before anyone tees off—that he's better than the rest of the sad sacks in the group, and despite the fact that he'll shoot a pretty average game he'll be giving tips and pointers all day long like he's David Leadbetter: "You know, you should think about leveling your swing plane and loosening that death grip on your club." I just want to look at him and say, "Death grip? How about the one I'm about to put on your trachea? See this 2 iron here? Why, I oughta . . ." Next time you're stuck with a guy like this, let me know. I'd be happy to forward Uncle Luigi's phone number.

My Favorite Excuse

Golf is a fickle game. One day you're Tiger Woods, swinging like a pro and shooting the score of your life. Next day, you're in the woods, shanking every club in the bag—including your putter, and that's hard to do! From the absolute top of the world, we plummet to the basement of golf hell, all in the span of 18 holes. Whither goest thou, O sweet golf swing of mine? As far as I'm concerned, the two greatest mysteries of life are the capricious nature of the golf swing and those socks that disappear in the dryer.

I've now spent slightly more than half a century investigating these conundrums but have yet to discover a clue that might shed light on either one. In the end, I can live without the vanished socks, but the missing golf swing drives me bonkers. That mystery is impenetrable.

> As far as I'm concerned, the two greatest mysteries of life are the capricious nature of the golf swing and those socks that disappear in the dryer.

Or is it? It occurred to me the other day that perhaps I was looking for answers in the wrong place all these years. My revelation came on the 9th tee box, just after my wife topped her drive 20 yards semi-forward into a patch of deep rough. "Can you guys shut up when I'm about to hit?" she asked, none too lovingly, of my brother and me. "Sorry," we replied in unison, sheepishly turning to get back into our carts.

When she chunked her next shot 15 yards forward into another thick scrap of spinach—with me and my brother completely silent—she said, "The sun was in my eyes. I'll pick up." And it occurred to me that she was absolutely right. How could she possibly have hit that shot when the sun was in her eyes? What in the name of Beetlejuice was the course architect thinking when he designed that blasted hole? I mean, c'mon, the sun shines most every day, right? Can't you angle the hole in a different direction?

Judging from the avalanche of excuses—some plausible, most not—that I've heard from golfers over the years, there seems to be a reason for every slice and hook, every whiff and dribble, every chunk and top. From the best pros to the average golfer, we have a raft of excuses at the ready. To hear most of us talk, we personally have very little to do with our inconsistencies on the course. It's someone talking in our backswing, or the sun in our eyes, it's our mismatched socks. For the professionals, it's almost always the course conditions. In interview after interview—as those Golf Channel zealots among us can testify—we hear the poor soul who just finished his round double bogey talking in zombie-like recitation: "The pins were tough out there . . . . The rug was rolling 28 on the Stimp . . . . The guys who played early had no wind . . . . Before I teed off, my wife told me I'm a zombie and she wants a divorce so she can marry an actual human being." Whatever, dude!

What about your playing companion being *too friendly*? This warped reasoning—your playing partner being too damn friendly—is my favorite excuse of all time. Case in point: I was playing a round with a lesser-known PGA Tour professional named Mark Carnevale a few years ago, and somehow, by being excessively friendly, I apparently ruined his career. We were at my home course, Secession Golf Club, in Beaufort, South Carolina, just before the MCI Heritage Classic in nearby Hilton Head. Carnevale was an alternate trying to get into the tournament field and was interested in playing a practice round to stay sharp and hone his game in case he got the call to play.

Through sloppy negotiations with his caddy at the local margarita bar the previous evening, he had consented to join my group. Carnevale's résumé includes but one win, at the 1992 Chattanooga Classic, but since that is one more than I can claim, he was a celebrity to me. Although to him it may have been a practice round to stay tournament-fresh, I had lots of questions about his playing routine, his pending endorsement deal with Spalding, and his experiences in trying to make it big on the Tour. In other words, I was being friendly.

I was actually playing fairly well that day and thoroughly enjoying myself. Carnevale, on the other hand, was spraying the ball around the course, was often in the marshland, and soon became oddly quiet. He hit the ball a mile, to be sure, but that is not necessarily an advantage at position-oriented Secession.

On the 7th hole, as I was walking up the fairway asking him some question or other, his caddy pulled me aside. "Excuse me," he said, "but Mr. Carnevale has asked that you not speak to him while he's playing."

We're all so much better than our scores indicate, aren't we?

"Huh?" I replied. "He feels that you're distracting him, and that's why he's not playing well." "Oh, I see." I soberly stared at him the balance of the day, which didn't seem to help his wayward game. He still stunk the place up.

In the gravel parking lot after our round, I broke the uneasy silence when he handed me a crisp $50 for the bet I had won from him. "Thanks, Mark!" I said, too cheerily. "Hope I didn't bother you too much today!" He grumbled something incomprehensible, got in his Cadillac DeVille, and sped away. That's still my favorite excuse of all: You're being too friendly, so I'm playing like crap. I guess I pushed Carnevale over the edge that day, as he all but disappeared from the Tour thereafter.

In the bigger scheme of things, I can relate to his need to reason away his poor play. We're all so much better than our scores indicate, aren't we? I'm absolutely convinced, for example, that American Airlines bent my new Callaway FT-*i* Driver in the cargo hold of a recent flight back from Hawaii, and I've not been able to hit a fairway since.

Perfectly fitted for my particular flail, the driver had been delivered the day before my trip, and I could hardly wait to get on the golf course. During the entire flight across the Pacific, I was picturing in my mind the perfect ball flight off the clubface, that smart twirl of the club in my hands as I bent over quickly to recover my tee, the prospect of the ball splitting the fairway 240 yards out. Unbelievably, that is exactly what happened all four rounds I played in the islands. When I got back home, I couldn't hit a fairway, there was no smart twirl, and my scores soared. Damn American Airlines! What other reason could there be for my failings?

So, in the spirit of good reasons for bad play, I offer herewith a few of the best and most pathetic excuses I've heard recently. I'm sure there are a million others, and I'd love to hear yours. In the meantime, try a few of these on your foursome next time out:

- It's too quiet out here.
- I broke a fingernail.
- The squirrels were staring at me.
- I was thinking too much.
- I have a blister on my heel.
- My spikes need tightening.
- I forgot to eat.
- The sun was in my eyes.

- I was thinking about world hunger.
- You're breathing too loudly.
- The tuna I ate for lunch must have been full of mercury.
- You're talking in my backswing.
- You're being too friendly.
- I think I saw Catherine Zeta-Jones in the parking lot.
- My favorite socks disappeared in the dryer.

CHAPTER

43

Top 10 New Year's Resolutions For Golfers

Since it's often too frigid for sane people to get in a round, winter tends to be a time of deep reflection, both in our personal lives and in our golf games. We look back at the past year and gaze forward into the new one. Being prone to introspection, we ask ourselves far-reaching, all-important questions, such as "Why did I drink so much eggnog and rum last night?" and "How many dimples are on a golf ball, anyway?"

Now I'd hate to have you stop reading here and waste your time counting, so before you go digging in your bag for a Titleist, let me give you the answer to the second question: Golf balls have between 300 and 500 dimples; common numbers are 336, 380, and 432.

In addition to pondering such questions, golfers—like everyone else on this rotating spheroid we call home—seem inclined to make New Year's resolutions. After all the "Be a better person," "Get involved in meaningful causes," and "Stop drinking so much eggnog and rum" vows, our resolutions—realistic or not—often pertain to our sorry golf games.

My guess is that most of us are not foolish enough to presume that practice makes perfect in golf. In fact, one look at our pathetic floundering on the tee box will disprove that theory beyond a reasonable doubt. On the other hand, I'd be surprised if most of us didn't harbor just a modest bit of hope that we can—maybe, possibly, one day soon—improve. It's not asking too much, is it? So why not resolve to do so now, this year. And while we're at it, let's decide at this very moment to satisfy all our other longstanding desires.

Curious as to what were the most common New Year's resolutions golfers make, I consulted two club professionals, Brad Apple and Jim McGurk of Spanish Trail Golf and Country Club in Las Vegas, who, I reasoned, must be experts in vows and resolutions, being that they're based in Las Vegas and all. With a combined 50 years in the golf industry, these guys have no doubt heard just about every resolution a golfer could possibly muster. (Those resolutions involving strippers, excess drinking, and binge gambling were excluded from their summary at my request.)

> I'd be surprised if most of us didn't harbor just a modest bit of hope that we can—maybe, possibly, one day soon—improve.

McGurk, a professional instructor and director of golf instruction at Spanish Trail, said, "Year after year, golfers make resolutions to improve things specific to their golf game. As an instructor, I like to know what their specific goals are, as this information provides me with a good starting point when working together. Some resolutions, however, are out of our hands. After all, I'm not a weight loss counselor!" Apple, Spanish Trail's resident golf professional, concurs, "Golfers tend to be somewhat goal-driven when it comes to their game, just by nature; so they tend to make resolutions each year. Some resolutions we can help with, and on others we just wish them well."

The two gentlemen kindly compiled a list for us of the 10 most common golf resolutions they've heard over the years. Most, they say, are achievable with the proper investment of time or money. Others require a little luck. (The commentary at the end of each is mine.)

Top 10 New Year's Resolutions for Golfers

10. Make a hole in one. (Remember what we said about luck?)

9. Take a golf trip. (Most common destinations: Ireland, Scotland.)

8. Go to the Masters. (Don't wait for a gilded invite from Tiger.)

7. Learn to hit a bunker shot. (Or any shot.)

6. Buy a new set of clubs. (Preferably from Brad—the commissions are good.)

5. Break 100, 90, 80, or 70 for the first time. (Meanwhile, hell is freezing over.)

4. Lower the handicap. (Meanwhile, pigs are flying.)

3. Take golf lessons. (Buy five and use one; most people do.)

2. Practice more. (Typically forgotten by January 2.)

1. Lose weight. (Golfers are people too—people who drink a lot of eggnog and rum.)

The Power of the Pen

Golf writers, like movie stars, are besieged by adoring fans. I can't tell you how many times I've been stopped at my local convenience store—arms loaded with a six-pack of Coors, a couple bags of Doritos, a tub of French onion dip, and my daily dose of Ding Dongs—by someone pleading for an autograph. And just imagine me trying to get through an airport! Impossible. Like Brad Pitt, I try everything—sunglasses, hoodies, outlandish hats—but nothing seems to work. My face is universally known, and the power of my pen just short of almighty.

Maybe adulation is simply a function of such uncontrollable fame. Here's a case in point: I was teeing it up in Hawaii one time a few years ago with Marlon Brando, Jack Nicholson, and Mick Jagger. Quite a foursome, eh? But the only guy who had to fend off fans was me. I'd hit a shot, swat away some fans, stroke a putt, and then run from a crowd. How in the world can a guy play golf like that?

> Golf writers, like movie stars, are besieged by adoring fans. . . . My face is universally known, and the power of my pen just short of almighty.

My mail and e-mail load is tremendous. In order to get any work—such as writing the eloquent essays in this book for your eternal enjoyment—done at all I need to take certain precautions. Often, I even need to cloak myself from my clingy family.

Consider the following exchange with my sister Vicki, who felt compelled to CC my other sister, Georgia:

> ```
> Little Bro,
>     The next time you speak with Edie, would
>     you ask her if she is planning anything
>     for David's 60th birthday? Maybe we can
>     treat him to a round of golf somewhere
>     nice. It takes considerable planning to
>     get out of this part of the world, so any
>     advance notice would be much appreciated.
>     Thank you!
>
> Love to you and Landry,
> V.
> ```

When I received this seemingly innocuous email from Vicki, I was in the midst of crafting a stirring retelling of a tale about Greg Norman and me on the island of Anguilla for a national and very important magazine. So I replied to Vicki and Georgia with what I hoped would be an off-putting reply that would close down communication immediately.

> ```
> Dear V.,
>     Mr. Fuller thanks you for being in touch
>     by e-mail. As much as he'd like to answer
>     all of his adoring fans personally,
>     he wants you to know that he receives
>     such an overwhelming quantity of daily
>     correspondence that it is impossible
>     for him to give personal attention to
>     each message (except those from Scarlett
>     Johansson, of course).
> ```

Mr. Fuller offers his most sincere and heartfelt thanks for your understanding. Please continue to buy his magazines, books, calendars, and forthcoming fragrance—Eau du Divot (available this fall in golf ball-shaped dispensers). If your request is urgent, Mr. Fuller *does* accept appointments via videoconference for a small fee of $2,500 for 15 minutes. Thanks so much.

Haley Hitemstraight
Personal (and I mean *very* personal)
Assistant to George Eliot Fuller III

But no, that only opened the door for another e-mail—this time from Georgia.

Dear Ms. Hitemstraight,
Does Mr. Fuller offer a family discount on the videoconference? This request concerns only immediate family, of course, and Ms. McGreal is proud to admit she is immediate family to Mr. Fuller. Thank you in advance for your prompt response.

Venus Lagputt
Personal (*not* so very) Assistant to Ms. Georgia Eliot Fuller McGreal, CLA, LMT

So I thought perhaps an even stronger reply would do the trick.

Dear Ms. Lagputt,
　Your e-mail was forwarded to me as head
of security for George Eliot Fuller
III Enterprises Inc. (a Cayman Island
corporation). Your attempts to invade
Mr. Fuller's privacy with your claims of
familial affiliation have caused concern.

In the interest of Mr. Fuller's safety,
please understand this is not the 1960s,
when girls could throw themselves at
his feet every time he appeared in
public. We have instituted a rigorous
identity-checking system. At Mr. Fuller's
request, please place all of your
personal belongings in 16-ounce plastic
bags (liquids in containers no larger
than 3 ounces) and FedEx them to us for
screening. Please also include two forms
of identification, which may include a
valid passport, driver's license, or
library card.

There is a small charge of $750 for us to
process and clear the items, after which
time we will pass along your request for
videoconferencing (at a discounted rate)
to Mr. Fuller's very personal assistant's
assistant, Becky Thatsgood. Any further
attempt to contact this office without
following the aforementioned procedures

will result in our filing attempted
trespassing and attempted assault
charges, even if the infractions are only
imaginary.

Not so sincerely,
James "Bulldog" Obee
Head of Security, George Eliot Fuller
III Enterprises Inc. (a Cayman Island
corporation)

But far from settling matters, that effort prompted the following reply.

Dear Bully,
(I trust you won't object to the more
familiar reference—I can readily imagine
you might be affectionately known as
"Bully", rather than the more formal
"Bulldog.") Most regrettably, Ms. McGreal
does not possess a valid passport,
although she does have an invalid passport
purchased in Tijuana several years ago.
The picture is a pretty good match.
Her driver's license was revoked due to
alleged connections to a small terrorist
cell and the fear that she might one day
offer to serve as the driver of a car
bomb.

She does, however, have two valid
library cards, one issued in Sacramento,

California, and the other in Honolulu,
Hawaii. Will these suffice as proper
identification? She carries no containers
of liquids greater than 3 ounces. We
question the need for such security
measures for a videoconference, but
please do apply the reduced family rate
to a videoconference with Mr. Fuller.
Ms. McGreal would be happy to prove
her assertion of family relationship by
way of potentially embarrassing photos.
Furthermore, from the closing sentence
in your last communication, we gather
that Mr. Fuller is still suffering the
occasional hallucinatory flashback, perhaps
from the glory days of the 1960s, and
extend our best wishes for a speedy
recovery.

Dick Cameupshort
Internet Security Advisor to Ms. McGreal,
CLA, LMT

I sensed I was losing the battle, not to mention that half the
day had been wasted in what Vicki seemed to feel was a fruitless
conversation.

You both have too much time on your
hands!!!!! :) :) :) :) :) (I'm not so sure
I'd admit the immediate family part!)

As you can see, my sister Vicki likes exclamation points and
smiley faces. Can you blame me for taking precautions? Still, in
the interest of getting back to work, I finally wrote back.

Vicki, I'd be happy to see what's planned for Dave's 60th. Maybe I can arrange a nice round at Torrey Pines. I'll catch up soon.

G.

And back to work I went, to continue exercising the power of the pen.

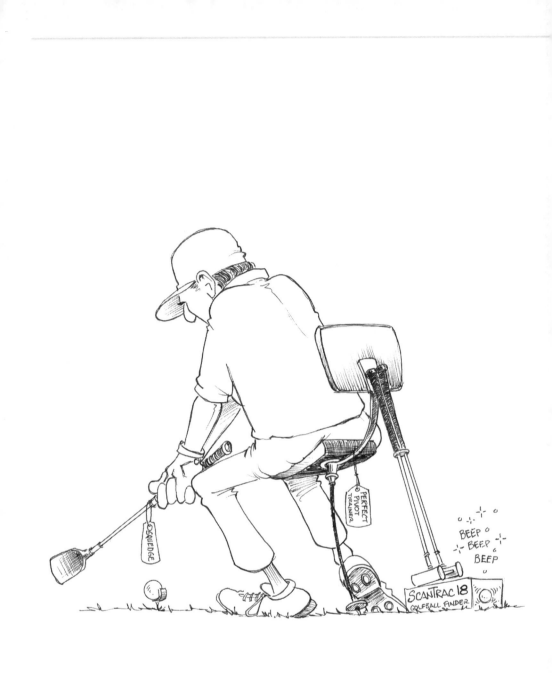

Beam Me Out of the Woods, Scotty

All hail good old-fashioned American ingenuity! It's what makes this country great and powerful and resilient. Who could deny the obvious design superiority of a country that invented the telephone, the automobile, the electric garage door, and the Flowbee haircutting system? Why I've even seen a spray-on hair product recently advertised on—say, didn't we invent the television, too?

This same ingenuity is also on display in golf. Americans are more than happy to allow the Scots (or Dutch, or Chinese, or Venezuelans, for that matter) to claim the invention of the magnificent old game. But as for its technological advancement, America is the hands-down world leader. As true as this is with clubs and balls from the major manufacturers, it's equally true with widgets, gadgets, instructional devices, and most every other tool (purported or actual) of the game.

Those of us in the serious golf press receive notice of hundreds of these innovative new products every year. A few even show up at the front door. Not only are we thus kept abreast of the latest developments in the marketplace, but also we are provided with hours of entertainment during those (rare) lull times—that is, when we're not mooching another free round of golf somewhere while wearing another free shirt.

One of the more revolutionary products I recently received was the Talking Putting Green, designed for your office or living room. This smart-alecky device boos and hisses your bad putts, oohs and aahs your near-misses, and magnanimously applauds when you drop a putt. "Our customers tell us this is the greatest golf gift idea they have seen in years," says the company-who-invented-it's president. Uh-huh.

Another of my favorites is the plastic tee with a vertical plastic shield on one side, a "unique design that keeps your club from ever actually touching the ball," according to the company's literature. This, it promises, will prevent sidespin and topspin, thus giving you that elusive, down-the-middle swat every single time. Of course, if you really want to

> This smart-alecky device boos and hisses your bad putts, oohs and aahs your near-misses, and magnanimously applauds when you drop a putt.

eliminate the flaws in your game, consider ordering an Iron Byron—that club-testing device used by the USGA—and you'll never again even have to swing the club.

Then there was the Squedge, a 55-degree loft wedge that's shaped like a kitchen spatula. Natch! Why didn't someone think of this before? The only mistake the manufacturers of this product made is not advertising the full potential of this club: When you're done on the golf course, just wipe it off and take it home to flip pancakes or swat flies.

Of course, I'd be remiss if I didn't tell you about former touring pro Jerry Heard's magnificent offer. He wrote, "Dear A.G. Links, You were referred to me as a serious golfer. Therefore I have selected you as one of a very restricted group of golfers to receive this offering." A.G. Links? So once I got past not being called by my name, I wondered where I could sign up for the trip-to-Vegas-if-only-I-buy-this-set-of-encyclopedias-or-insurance-premium.

Instead of encyclopedias or insurance, however, Jerry wanted to know if I (or Mr. Links, whom he had so personally selected) was interested in being among the "very limited number of golfers who will ever know the esoteric superior golf knowledge that makes up the secrets of the big money golf pros." By this time, I'm practically panting. I do, Jerry, I do. Esoteric superior golf knowledge is my life's purpose. How did you know? If I order now, do I get a set of Ginsu steak knives? And you were probably wondering where Jerry Heard had gotten off to.

> Esoteric superior golf knowledge is my life's purpose. How did you know? If I order now, do I get a set of Ginsu steak knives?

On the actual game improvement side of American inventiveness is the Pendulum Putter, a product with not one, but two—count 'em, two—shafts. This "unique [funny how that word keeps popping up in promotional literature] dual shaft construction is designed to correct some of the biggest problems faced by all golfers. By separating the hands on two shafts, the muscles of the hands and wrists are eliminated, making it extremely difficult to push or pull a putt." On the other hand, I'd wager that we could figure out some way to miss our putts anyway. Five bucks on it?

I recently received the as a sample something called the Golf Club Scrub Brush. For only $16.99 (get 'em while they last!), I can purchase a highly sophisticated tool for doing what a wet towel will do for $0—clean my golf club. I'm not sure how I've managed for the past 50 years without one. Now I look at my stinky old towel and think, "Pshaw! You nasty rag!" As a special bonus, one side of my new club scrubber is made of steely wires suitable for cleaning my barbeque grill at home. And the invention beat goes on . . . .

The Perfect Pivot Golf Swing Trainer looks like a pretty legitimate tool. The concept is simple: It's a bicycle seat mounted on a monopod with a back support similar to a receptionist's chair. Step right up and sit right down. Now this might feel a little funny at first—getting a wedgie and perfecting your wedgies at the same time—but believe me, it'll do you a lot of good. "The Perfect Pivot holds your body in position from setup through impact. After impact, the spinal support 'springs' you upward and onto your forward foot." Fun, but do you really care about improving your game that much?

The game improvement device that I've yet to get a clear picture of is described like this: "A strap binds the left foot at one end, the right knee at the other. The player hobbles a few steps forward for the swing. As the club descends toward the ball, the shaft suddenly springs like a rubber band." They sent no photos of this one, and the only question I have about it is this: When does the lady in the leather suit with the whip show up to make sure I keep my left arm straight?

Next, I'm expecting someone to send me a straightjacket that will train me to keep my arms still while swinging . . . from the rafters. Can I get the matching hood and ball gag? There's a whole arena of merchandise just waiting to be invented for us sicko golfers.

Finding lost golf balls is another big theme for inventors. The most stupendous new product ever developed for this purpose, the Scantrack 18 Golfball Finder, works on the following principle: Every object in the universe emits a distinct electromagnetic pulse. That pulse is intensified when the object is struck by a blunt weapon such as a golf club. It used to be that when the result of the blow was a flight of the object into the woods, the golfer would utter some expletives, hitch up his silly-looking trousers, and stalk over to waste 5 minutes of his time desperately seeking his Club Special.

No more! Technology has now been developed to find that irritating little ball no matter where it goes. A microchip inserted into a handheld device about the size of a television remote control will follow the electromagnetic pulse of the freshly struck golf ball and an antenna will point in the direction the signal is coming from. By following the zagging line of the antenna, you will eventually be staring once again at your wayward friend, the golf ball. Beam me out of the woods, Scotty. You might look pretty silly using it, but if it works, who cares?

Once again American ingenuity proves an age-old principle: For every sensible invention there is at least one equal and opposite stupid one. On the other hand, I can hardly wait to open my mail every day.

Afterword: My Next Book

My Dear Reader,

I hope that you have thoroughly enjoyed the stories and musings in the preceding pages, laughed out loud a few times, smiled throughout, and maybe even learned a thing or two along the way. And while this current tome is blissfully devoid of instruction of any kind, my next book will address exactly that subject. I must confess up front that I am completely unqualified to provide advice of this nature—or, probably, advice of *any* nature, to be honest—but I nonetheless thought you'd appreciate a sneak peek at my chapter outlines and the opportunity to order a copy in advance.

I heartily promise my next effort will be unlike any instruction book you've ever read. You certainly won't learn grip or stance fundamentals, no balance or posture techniques, nothing whatsoever about swing planes or angles of descent. There will be no chapters on wrist-free putting or proper sand shot execution. In fact, I postulate that you should avoid lessons and practice at all costs, cease reading all those conflicting theories in instructional magazines, play as frequently as you can, and learn as you go. Plus, my next book will be chock-full of useful tips on staying calm on the golf course during the long years of strife, struggle, and aggravation you're bound to endure by following my teachings.

I've patented my approach and, accordingly, have named my book *The Trial and Error, Error, Error, Error . . . Method*. The projected list price of *TT&EEEE . . . M* is only US$49,995.99 per copy, and I encourage you to order it immediately. By the time I'm done writing it, the costs may have soared, but I'll still let you have it for the price quoted here.

If I could sell just one or two books up front, I'd be most appreciative. The money would go a long way toward funding the years of green fees required for me to write the book in the first place. I think you will agree that, due to the vast research involved, the price is very fair. Don't wait! Please order before I have to get a real job! Thank you so much in advance for your undying support, patience, and generosity. (Note: No Ginsu steak knives are included with each order.)

The Trial and Error, Error, Error, Error . . . Method Proposed Table of Contents

Foreword: Shut Up and Stop Complaining, by Mick Murphy, author of the best-selling *Murphy's Law*

Chapter 1   **How to Properly Line Up Your Fourth Putt**

Plus: Making everyone on the golf course wait while you line up your quadruple bogey putt from every conceivable angle

Chapter 2   **How to Hit a Nike From the Rough When You Hit a Titleist From the Tee**

Plus: Rounding down your score to assuage your ego

Chapter 3   **How to Avoid the Water When You Lie 8 in a Bunker**

Plus: Simple solutions to the problem of caring too much about a round

Chapter 4   **How to Get More Distance off the Shank**

Plus: The joys of the foot wedge

Chapter 5   **When to Yell at the Ranger**

Plus: Deliberately slowing play to anger the group behind you

Chapter 6 **Using Your Shadow on the Greens to Maximize Earnings**

Plus: Coughing, unfastening Velcro, and other gamesmanship techniques

Chapter 7 **Techniques for Throwing Clubs Without Hurting Yourself**

Plus: Guide on retrieving clubs stuck in tree branches

Chapter 8 **Believable Excuses for Drinking Before 9 a.m.**

Plus: A primer on mixing golf cart cocktails

Chapter 9 **How to Rationalize a Six-Hour Round**

Plus: The FAQs on making citizen's arrests

Chapter 10 **How to Find a Ball That Everyone Else Saw Go Into the Water**

Plus: Guide to common waterfowl on the golf courses of North America

Chapter 11 **Why Your Spouse Doesn't Care That You Birdied the 5th**

Plus: Ordering pizza delivery to the 10th tee

Chapter 12 **How to Let a Foursome Play Through Your Twosome**

Plus: Why you should never pick up on a hole, even when you lie 12

Chapter 13 **How to Relax When You Are Hitting Three Off the Tee**

Plus: Surefire methods for overcorrecting a slice with a duck hook

Chapter 14 When to Suggest Major Swing Corrections to Your Opponent

Plus: A look at golf fashion from 1960 to 1975, and when to wear plaid with stripes

Chapter 15 When to Regrip Your Ball Retriever

Plus: A look at Web sites that sell recovered golf balls

Chapter 16 God and the Meaning of the Birdie-to-Bogey Three-Putt

Plus: The spiritual side of never breaking 100

So there you have it, dear reader, everything you ever wanted to know about how to play the game of golf. Order now and remember it's not whether you win or lose that counts, but how cool you can be when playing the game. Best to all, and hit 'em straight (if you can)!

George Fuller

Reference Points

Chapter 3

Page 11: "practice, quite unofficial, of allowing. . .": Dobereiner, P. and B. Elliot. 2005. *Golf rules explained.* 11th ed. Devon, UK: David and Charles.

Page 11: "I don't even know if . . .": Davies, P. 2005. *The historical dictionary of golfing terms: from 1500 to present.* 4th ed. Lincoln, NE: Bison Books.

Page 12: Smith, D.L. 1984. *Winged foot story: the golf, the people, the friendly trees.* Mamaroneck, NY: Winged Foot Golf Club.

Chapter 4

Page 17: Golf Nut Society, www.golfnuts.com.

Page 17: "after he skipped the ceremony . . .": Lieberman, P. 2008. Think you're a contender for Golf Nut of the Year? *Los Angeles Times* February 7, 2008. http://articles.latimes.com/2008/feb/07/nation/na-golfnutlist7/.

Chapter 6

Page 27: "Them golfs must be some tough critters . . .": "The Clampetts and the Dodgers." 10 Apr 1963. *The Beverly Hillbillies.* CBS.

Chapter 7

Page 33: "The DoubleWall has been independently tested . . .": Pinemeadow Golf, www.pinemeadowgolf.com/golf-clubs/woods/doublewall/.

Page 33: "thinned the face of the 3DX DC . . ." Nickent Golf, www.nickentgolf.com/pr_iw_3dx_dc-01/.

Chapter 15

Page 71: "I have very poor eyesight . . .": In Golf We Trust. 13 May 2007. *90 year-old man scores hole-in-one.* http://www.ingolfwetrust.com/golf-central/2007/05/13/90+YearOld+Man+Scores+HoleInOne.aspx.

Chapter 16

Page 74: "an advanced personal energy system": QeShop, http://www.qeshop.com/Qlink.aspx?PromoID=QLINKOFFER&sku=0101.

Chapter 18

Page 85: "At the deepest level . . .": Chopra, D. 2003. *Golf for enlighten-ment: The Seven Lessons for the Game of Life*. New York: Harmony.

Chapter 19

Page 88: "Since I'm a long hitter . . .": Shark.com. Tip #7: get inside their head. http://www.shark.com/sharkwatch/instruction/tip7.php

Page 89: "I love it if it's done fairly . . .": Kessler, P. 2007. www.golfonline.com/golfonline/features/kessler/columnist/0,17742,482639,00.html

Chapter 20

Page 93: "Do you currently dive in the ponds . . .": ReTeeGolf, http://home.nc.rr.com/reteegolf/index.htm.

Chapter 22

Page 100: "the trash, the whole trash . . .": Trashmasters, www.trash-masters.com

Page 101: "I'm not sure I'm really going . . .": Husband, B. Former vice-president gets trashed in Snowmass. *The Aspen Times*. Quoted at http://www.trashmasters.com/articles/former_vp_gets_trashed.html

Chapter 24

Page 111: "What you focus on . . .": Dr. J. Mitchell Perry at a seminar attended by the author.

Page 111: "Once you address the golf ball . . .": Penick, H. 1992. *Harvey Penick's little red book*. New York: Simon & Schuster.

Chapter 26

Page 119: "pickled genitalia, minced eyelids, and shredded nostrils . . .": Feherty, D. 2003. *A nasty bit of rough*. New York: Rugged Land.

Chapter 34

Page 157: "We all grew up watching . . .": Loudmouth Golf, www.loud-mouthgolf.com.

Chapter 36

Page 165: "The extroverted Demaret kidded . . .": Seitz, N. April 2000. Living out loud. *Golf Digest*.

Chapter 37

Page 170: "You know how to whistle . . .": *To Have and Have Not*. 1944. Dir. Howard Hawks. Screenplay by Jules Furthman and William Faulkner. Warner Bros. Pictures.

Page 171: "Any golfer caught whistling . . .": Wood, D. The original rules of golf revisited. www.cybergolf.com/golf_news/the_original_rules_of_golf_revisited.

Chapter 39

Page 182: "trained his setters to hunt . . .": 28 March 1909. Dogs hunt golf balls. *The New York Times.*

Page 182: "herd and harass, but never harm": Geese Police, www.geese-policeinc.com.

Chapter 40

Page 187: Associated Press. 23 December 1995. Golfer dies after hole-in-one. *The New York Times.*

Chapter 41

Page 190: "freaks along the fairway": Zuckerman, J. 2006. *Misfits on the links.* Kansas City: Andrews McMeel Publishing.

About the Author

George Fuller is publisher and editor in chief of *Tee It Up* magazine (geared to golfers in Southern California) and partner to a nationally syndicated radio show of the same name. He has been in the publishing business, specializing in travel and golf, for more than 15 years and has been a professional writer for more than 20 years, using his humor to add a perspective that has proven popular with his readers.

Fuller has authored eight books; the most recent two are *California Golf: The Complete Guide* and *Discover Hawaii's Best Golf*. He also has an online following, serving as the regular golf travel correspondent for CBS Sportsline. Former editor in chief of *Links—The Best of Golf* magazine and founder of *Golf Living* magazine, Fuller has contributed to many respected newspapers and magazines, including *Robb Report*, the *Wall Street Journal*, *San Francisco Chronicle*, the *Los Angeles Times*, *Time* magazine, *Golf* magazine, *Travel & Leisure Golf*, *Links—The Best of Golf* magazine, and *Coastal Living*. Fuller resides in Culver City, California.

About the Illustrator

Joe Jahraus worked for many years in advertising management positions at Ralston Purina, Skelly Oil, and Getty Oil. He also served as creative director at Hallmark Cards for Hallmark's line of humorous greeting cards. In the late '80s, Jahraus turned his passion for cartooning into a full-time business, becoming a participant in many of the leading arts and crafts festivals throughout the United States. In recent years, he and his son, Jon, developed and operate a gift-buying Web site (www.netoons.com), where they create and personalize cartoon orders for customers world-wide. Jahraus resides with his wife, Sharon, and dog, Sam, in Broken Arrow, Oklahoma.